The voice of the consumer is at the heart of any great marketing. Cheers to Michele for a smart, simple guide to help leaders hear the consumer and turn insights into action.

- Cathy Lanning,
Vice President, Strategic Partnerships, Nationwide Insurance

I wish I had a copy of this book as a young marketer or business student. A book like this would have been invaluable and prevented a number of learn as you go mistakes on my part.

- Ray Thomson,
Executive Vice President, Global Marketing, Huffy Bicycles

Focus groups are an integral part to gaining consumer insight and understanding. A copy of Michele's book should be in every marketer's toolbox.

- Tim Martin,
General Manager & Vice President, Scotts Miracle-Gro

This book provides a clear, succinct, real-world approach to focus groups. It should be considered a must-read primer for any new brand manager. Being a key stakeholder in focus group research will serve you well over many years, as you will be garnering valuable insights for your brands.

- Nancy DeMuch,
Vice President Marketing, JP Morgan Chase

If I'd never attended a focus group (let alone planned one), I'd know exactly what I was in for with the picture this book painted in my mind.

- Michelle Claravall,
Menu Innovation Manager, McDonald's Corporation

Kudos for an easy-to-read and easy-to-understand basics-of-focus-groups book that demystifies this qualitative research tool.

- Dana Conover,
Former Director Marketing, Innovation, Elmer's Products

This will be a useful tool for not only brand managers, but also market research managers, who have not done a lot of focus groups.

- Cindy Dyer,
Former Director Market Research, Abbott Nutrition

Focus Groups 101

The Brand Marketer's Guide to
The 5 Stages of Focus Group Research

Michele L Brenner

Copyright © 2016 Michele L Brenner
All rights reserved.

In accordance with the U.S. Copyright Act of 1976, the scanning, uploading, and electronic sharing of any part of this book without the permission of the publisher constitute unlawful piracy and theft of the author's intellectual property. If you would like to use material from the book (other than for review purposes), prior written permission must be obtained by contacting the author at www.focusgroups101.com.

Thank you for your support of the author's rights.

The examples in this book come out of the author's two decades of work in consumer brand marketing and marketing research. In order to protect the intellectual property of many businesses and brands, identifying details have been changed.

First Edition

ISBN: 978-1537046068

*This book is dedicated to my family
for their love and support.*

*Steve, Olivia, Owen & Jack,
you are my dreams come true.*

Contents

Preface: What This Book Will Do For You 1

Focus Group Case Study: No More Guilt—
I'll Decide How To Feed My Puppy 5

Part One—Market Research Methodologies 7

- Consumer Insights, Formerly Known As
  Market Research 9
- Case Study of When To Use Qualitative Research 14
- Qualitative Research Methodologies 16

**Part Two—The Brand Marketer's Guide to
The 5 Stages of Focus Group Research** 23

Stage 1: Write the Research Brief 25

Stage 2: Recruit the Participants 38

Stage 3: Develop the Discussion Guide & Stimuli 45

Stage 4: Conduct the Research 62

Stage 5: Analyze & Share the Research Results 70

Acknowledgements 76

Resource List 78

Bonus Content 79

- Essays from Ruth Connolly, Marty Johnson
  and Kendall Nash 81
- Sample documents: 100
  - Research Brief 100

About The Author 104

Visit www.focusgroups101.com
for other FREE sample focus group documents.

Preface:
What This Book Will Do For You

I built my career in consumer products marketing at Campbell's Soup Company, Scotts Miracle-Gro, and a former New York advertising agency, working on Procter & Gamble's Clearasil skincare brand. In all that time, understanding how the consumer thinks was always the most interesting part of marketing to me.

After more than ten years now as an independent marketing and market research consultant, I have conducted focus groups on all sorts of topics with many different participants. The process is second nature for me, but I was surprised that I couldn't find any how-to guides to share the process with my fellow marketers. That's why I set out to write this book.

The reason companies do market research in the first place is **we are not our consumers**. Marketers typically live and work in places that do not represent the "average" consumer. It's no wonder one of the biggest mistakes marketers can make is assuming our own motivations mirror those of the people who buy our products and services.

Focus Groups 101 Michele L. Brenner

This book is for anyone who wants to understand how to conduct focus group research to make better consumer-informed business decisions. Understanding consumers' perspectives will ultimately help marketers and other business leaders excel in their own careers by allowing them to create products, services and messages that best meet consumers' needs and desires.

Many new brand managers, and other business people outside of the marketing function, are given the responsibility of "doing focus groups" without much training on how best to do it. Reading this book will prepare you to approach your next focus group project confident you are well informed.

Meant to be a quick read, this book is intended to feel more like satisfying a curiosity than studying for an exam.

In Part One, the book explains and gives pros and cons of several research methodologies and the best applications for each. I will give a broad overview of the **two main types of market research, quantitative and qualitative**. Then we will delve into specific *qualitative*

Preface: What This Book Will Do For You

methodologies and, finally, move into the meat of the book on how to conduct successful focus groups.

I am a fan of focus groups as a research methodology for several reasons. The researcher is able to ask follow up questions to probe the reasons *why* people give the answers they do. Talking "live" with consumers gives the researcher an opportunity not only to listen to what the consumers are saying, but also to notice the level of engagement behind the consumers' comments and to read their body language. Focus groups allow you to talk to more people in a shorter amount of time than one-on-one interviews, which saves time *and* money.

From a business' perspective, it is ideal to bring team members from multiple functions together in the backroom to listen to and watch the consumers "live". I have found it is easier for companies to mobilize behind the results of research when people from a few departments and levels of management have heard the same thing at the same time. Observing focus groups together also provides the side benefit of team building.

Part Two contains **The Brand Marketer's Guide to the 5 Stages of Focus Group Research**. The process provided in this book for managing a focus group project can be applied more broadly to many qualitative research methodologies.

The 5 Stages of Focus Group Research are:
1. Write the Research Brief
2. Recruit the Participants
3. Develop the Discussion Guide and Stimuli
4. Conduct the Research
5. Analyze and Share the Research Results

Having lived both sides, I hope this book will help build a stronger connection between the marketing and market research functions. Focus groups are one form of qualitative market research. Market research overall exists to mitigate business risk and maximize business potential by cultivating understanding of what motivates the end users of products and services. In the end, it's all about selling more stuff, but it's doing it by providing what the consumer needs or desires when and where they want it, not by "pushing" more stuff at them.

Whether you are doing a focus group study yourself or working with a qualitative research supplier, understanding the five stages of managing a focus group project will help make your research more effective, more efficient, and more actionable for your business. Over time, this will lead to more sales and ultimately more success in your marketing career.

Focus Group Research Case Study:

No More Guilt—I'll Decide How to Feed My Puppy

Puppy food is expensive, so it is not surprising many new puppy owners are turning to generic versions of their branded favorites. My branded puppy food client was interested in showing print advertising concepts to new puppy owners who fed generic puppy food to their zero to six month old puppies.

The goal of the advertising was to encourage new puppy owners feeding generic puppy food to switch back to branded puppy food. The general theme of the ad concepts was "don't compromise." The ads showed many situations in which it was just as good to use something sort of like the original product—using old towels, second-hand puppy Halloween outfits, pre-owned dog beds, etc. The ads went on to say that nutrition for your growing, developing puppy was not one of those areas where it was okay to compromise.

These advertising-like concepts—think rough print ads—were shown to new puppy owners over a couple days in one Midwestern market in groups of three people (triads). Smaller groups enabled the opinions and perceptions of the new puppy owners to be explored in more depth than larger groups would allow.

Shockingly to the ad agency, the "don't compromise" concept of the ads was off-putting to these new puppy owners. The owners had compared ingredients of the generics to the branded puppy food and many of their veterinarians had even suggested generic puppy food to them.

The owners felt it was offensive for the leading puppy food brand to suggest that they would feed their new puppies something less than optimal nutrition. There were dog owners with tear-rimmed eyes telling me they would *never* compromise on their new puppy's nutrition. The brand telling them generics meant compromise went against their well-meaning, value-conscious ideals.

Ultimately, the client decided to take another route, choosing to avoid the potential negative impact on overall brand perceptions should that ad campaign have gone to market.

A focus group cynic could say that this was an unfair killing of a creative idea based on the feedback of only twenty-four new puppy owners. On the other hand, my perception was that the new puppy owners articulated concerns the brand team had all along but hadn't quite been able to put into words to communicate to the ad agency. The brand team was very happy with the research findings and was pleased to avoid any ill will against the brand.

Part One — Marketing Research Methodologies

Explanation of Select Terms:

What's the difference between Market Research and Marketing Research?

Market research refers to the investigation of the market, which could include products, brands, competitors, distribution outlets and consumers themselves. Marketing Research is the investigation of the impact of any element of the marketing mix, including Product, Price, Place or Promotion. In practice the terms are used interchangeably.

What's the difference between a Business Objective and a Research Objective?

A Business Objective is a measurable business goal. A Research Objective is a statement of what is to be learned. Research objectives should support a particular business objective. For example, a Business Objective may be to launch a new product in the next twelve months that will lead to more than a million dollars in annual profit. The supporting Research Objective could be to gauge the interest level of the brand's target consumers in several different new product concepts to help determine which new product to commercialize.

Who is the Client?

You will see the word "Client" used many times in this book. To whom "Client" refers depends heavily on the context in which it is used. There are many "Clients" in the world of marketing research, for example: The Focus Group Moderator who hires the Research Facility; The Market Research Manager who hires the Focus Group Moderator; The Brand Marketer for whom the Market Research Manager is coordinating the research; The Senior Executive at the top of the marketing organization in which the Brand Marketer works; the Board of Directors of the company where the Senior Executive works; Wall Street; and ultimately Jane or Joe Consumer.

Consumer Insights, Formerly Known As Market Research

The key to successful market research is to define the business objectives of the research, and then design a research plan that will get the learnings needed to help make those business decisions.

Before delving into how to conduct focus group research, it is important to understand the context for when focus groups are the best research methodology to use. The following section will discuss consumer insights in general and help the marketer decide which market research methodology is best for various business objectives.

Good consumer insights save a business more than they cost to develop.

Consumer Insights, also known as Market Research, is used to increase businesses' success with anything they have to offer—such as products, packaging, customer service, merchandising and advertising messages. Research is often used if a company is doing something new in the market or trying to sell to a new segment of consumers. Many large national brands also do research at regular intervals to see if perceptions of their brand or usage of the products is changing over time.

Consumer insights can reduce the chance of failure in the marketplace, thereby saving the company the cost of commercialization.

More often than not, the cost of a consumer insights project is well below the cost of a marketplace mistake.

Ponder this: In order to launch a new product, the business is going to have to invest resources in product development, packaging development, graphic design, messaging, manufacturing, sales and distribution. With that kind of investment—which can easily reach into the millions of dollars for a national brand—wouldn't you want a preview of how consumers are going to react to the new product or program?

You might also want to know whether there is anything you can do to optimize the product, packaging or messaging for the consumer. And you're certainly going to want to ensure that this new offering will not have any negative effects on your current business. As such, it makes sense to get feedback directly from consumers who you hope will be buying your product or service.

As a marketer, consumer research can also be valuable because the consumer insights can lend confidence in the marketing choices you will make. When you know you're doing something the consumer needs or wants it will build passion in your mission, which can help influence the rest of the business team.

Consumer Insights, Formerly Known As Market Research

Of course, each organization has its own tolerance level for risk and how much information it needs to feel comfortable to make decisions. This book provides a guide for making smart research choices based on my twenty-plus years of working in consumer products marketing. It is not a strict rulebook and I encourage business managers to consider their own business circumstances before enacting any of the processes I suggest in the book.

Qualitative *AND* Quantitative Research Have Roles in Consumer Insights.

There are two major types of Consumer Insights studies—*qualitative and quantitative*. Using focus groups is a common methodology for *qualitative* research.

Qualitative Research is used to understand consumers' perceptions, opinions, beliefs, attitudes, and language around a given topic. With qualitative research, you come away with stories in consumers' own words about the roles products or services play in their lives. This type of research is comprised of **mostly open-end questions, which aim to illuminate the reasons behind consumers' opinions**.

Qualitative research is interviewing done with fewer respondents and provides an opportunity for in-depth discussion to probe and build on consumer feedback in the moment. The learnings are used to refine ideas prior to quantitative research, or further development of the product, positioning, packaging or advertising.

A limitation, due to the low numbers of respondents involved, is the **results of qualitative research are considered "directional"** and not necessarily projectable to a broader population.

Often companies will start with qualitative research such as focus groups to uncover any hidden issues and learn the language of the consumer. After that it often makes sense to refine the offering and then do a quantitative study to get projectable purchase intent and source of volume results to make a final go/no-go decision.

Source: Yin Yang Symbol by Danilo Rizzuti

Consumer Insights, Formerly Known As Market Research

Quantitative research differs in that is done with large numbers of respondents, so the results are statistically significant and projectable across a larger population. This type of research is comprised of **mostly closed-end questions, such as multiple choice or rating scales**.

Because the research is done with so many respondents, it can be unwieldy to have many open-end questions, where answers would require more hands-on analysis. Another limitation is in quantitative research you **can't usually follow up with real-time probing questions** to fully understand consumers' answers.

If you're new to research, you can remember that "quant" sounds a bit like "count", and in quantitative it's all about the numbers. Quantitative research has many methodologies including central location testing, phone polls, simple online surveys, and more complex (usually online) methodologies like conjoint analysis, segmentation studies, etc.

Once a business knows the exact questions it needs to ask, **quantitative research can provide "hard data" on which to base business decisions**. It provides large amounts of data that help validate one strategy versus another. It can also work in the reverse order—a company could learn interesting facts from a quantitative study, which it then may want to understand more fully through qualitative research.

This book will concentrate specifically on focus groups and will not get into quantitative research other than this quick mention. In summary, **qualitative and quantitative methodologies have complementary strategic roles to play in market research**—businesses tend to get the most benefit when they do some of both types.

I caution that **no book can make up for the years of study and practice** of a market research professional. Throughout the book I will reference other books and resources for those readers who want to become skillful suppliers of focus group research.

Case Study Of When To Use *Qualitative* Research

A national laundry products brand wanted to update, refresh and generally contemporize its packaging. This brand had been selling laundry detergent in rectangular "boxy" bottles for decades. There was also an opportunity to use less plastic overall, thereby reducing the cost of the bottle.

In the early stages of this package design project, focus groups were conducted to understand what various bottle shapes from many different categories communicated to consumers.

For a few reasons, *qualitative* research was the methodology of choice in this instance. It was clear from those focus groups that bottles with curves were seen as more modern and up-to-date than rectangular bottles with harder angles. This was not something we would have been easily able to ask or understand in a multiple-choice question.

Also, at this point, no significant capital investments were needed. It wasn't necessary to have statistically reliable and projectable data to make sure we would have good ROI for capital spending. We needed to gain consumer understanding to help refine the creative direction provided to the package designers. That is to say that the cost risk was pretty low at this stage of the project.

Later in the project, when the business team was happy with the way the new bottle design looked and performed, it was an appropriate time to use *quantitative* research to confirm that the new bottle

Case Study Of When To Use Qualitative Research

shape would sell just as well or better than the old bottle. When you change a classic there's always a risk for hurting the business. Hundreds of thousands of dollars in new bottle manufacturing equipment were also riding on this decision. And it was a very clear yes or no question—would the new bottle sell well or not? For these reasons a quantitative study made sense at this point.

A study was done with hundreds of consumers from across the United States. In the test, consumers looked at an online image of a retail shelf stocked with laundry detergent bottles. From each shelf they chose which product they would most likely buy. Each consumer saw several different individual shelf images where variants such as bottle shape, price and brand were changed. Through the magic of mathematical equations—like regression analysis—the business team could predict with statistical certainty the new bottle design was a clear winner.

Qualitative Research Methodologies:

This section briefly describes four of the most common qualitative research methodologies, including focus groups, ethnography, shop-alongs, in-depth interviews—and a quick mention of the digital versions of all of these.

Focus Groups are when a moderator interviews groups of consumers together about a specific topic. For example, gaining mothers' feedback to several new product concepts for new nutritionally supplemented foods and beverages for toddlers. Other topics can include advertising or packaging feedback, product category behaviors and attitudes exploration, brand-positioning insights, feedback on product prototypes, and more.

These group discussions are typically both audio and video recorded. They are usually observed by a group of interested parties from a back room behind a one-way mirror. They can also be livestreamed so clients can "be there" without traveling.

Focus groups have many benefits. Participants build on each other's thinking which helps the marketer get a more robust picture of what consumers think. They are great for collecting consumer language around a topic and for understanding what is being communicated to consumers from any given stimulus, such as a new product concept, packaging graphics or advertising. They are also very good as follow-up to quantitative research to build understanding of why consumers responded to communication, product or service in a certain way.

Talking "live" with consumers gives the researcher an opportunity not only to listen to what the consumers are saying, but also to notice the level of engagement behind the consumers' comments and to read their body language. Talking to consumers in groups allows you to talk to more people in a shorter amount of time than one-on-one interviews, which saves time *and* money. Because of that time savings focus groups have a lower cost per respondent than individual interviews.

Let's look at a few big picture do's and don'ts for focus groups:

- *Do* use focus groups to find out what the stimuli (such as a new product concepts, advertising, packaging forms or packaging graphics) are communicating to consumers with the goal of further refining the stimuli.

- *Don't* use focus groups to approve or kill creative work based on consumer preference. Qualitative research is not designed to get feedback from enough people to be considered projectable to a larger population. Furthermore, qualitative research is best at helping you understand the *reasons behind* consumer preference, not the preference itself.

- *Don't* try to determine a specific optimal price of a product or service. Quantitative methodology is better for determining pricing. You *can*, however, use focus groups to learn whether consumers consider an offering premium or cost-effective or cheap compared to the current or competitive offerings.

- *Do* use a professional research recruitier. Professional recruiters have laboriously amassed large databases of consumers to get exactly who you want to talk to for your research.
    o In addition to pre-screening the participants, they also pro-

vide logistical instructions to respondents, plus remind and reconfirm respondents before the research. Recruiters will handle payments of respondent incentives, assign and follow up on homework, and deal with any participant issues.

- o Using a recruiting firm can also help keep the brand or company sponsoring the research anonymous to participants. This will help reduce respondents' biases and desire to please the audience behind the mirror.

- *Do* use an experienced professional focus group moderator to facilitate getting equal and unbiased feedback from all respondents in the face of participants who try to dominate the conversation or ones who need a little prodding to speak their minds.

- *Don't* allow the dominant personality in the group to take all the airtime or unduly influence others' opinions. A moderator should draw out the opinions of the quieter respondents. The research participants who take time to think before they speak often have interesting things to say.

- *Do* use an optimal group size to achieve your objectives. With smaller groups you can go more in-depth in a shorter amount of time. I like to talk with six to eight respondents in a two-hour focus group that has two or three main topics to cover. With ten respondents it limits the time for probing follow up questions, which will reduce the amount of new insights you can gain.

Ethnography, or individual interviews conducted within the context of consumers' lives (often their homes), is another useful qualitative research methodology, especially when you want to see how a product is used in a real life setting. Ethnography is particularly good for identifying needs consumers don't even recognize.

For example, for a food products company, I was involved in interviewing baby boomers at home to learn about their attitudes

Qualitative Research Methodologies:

and behaviors regarding food and nutrition. At-home interviews allowed discussion <u>and</u> observation of actual consumers' refrigerators, cupboards and pantry contents to give more context to the practices they reported.

A big benefit of ethnography is seeing what is *actually* in consumers' homes when hearing them describe what they do. It probably does not come as a shock to hear that what gets reported and what is observed does not always match. Like the woman who claims she eats organic whole foods, but is observed with a freezer stuffed with highly processed frozen meals. When you notice a disconnect like that and are right there with her in her kitchen, it's easy to ask who eats those frozen meals. You may learn she doesn't always have time to prepare organic, whole foods for herself. Or, you may find out that she buys the frozen meals for her teenage son.

These interviews do not have to happen inside the home. Other ethnographies I have done involved homeowners who fertilize their lawns, to observe how and where they stored their fertilizer spreader, as well as see it in action. These observations allowed for visual feedback on where there might be opportunities for improvement in making the spreader easier to store or use. Seeing homeowners operate their spreaders helped the product design engineers develop an easy way for consumers to activate the edge shield feature to keep fertilizer from being spread beyond the lawn onto their sidewalks or driveways.

One key consideration for ethnography is that the number of observers during the sessions has to be limited for space consideration, and so the participant will think, feel and act as close as possible to how they normally would in their own environment. The interviewer, videographer and other observers also dress to fit into the participant's environment, not as they would dress for the office.

Shop-Alongs are when a researcher observes and interviews pre-screened consumers while they shop. Shop-a-longs are **great reality**

checks for the marketer to see what *actually* catches the eye and what level of attention is paid at the shelf. Did he quickly scan to find his favorite brand or product, and then take it without looking at any of the other choices? Did she look at the labels of two or three products before making her choice? What part of the labels was she spending the most time studying?

They can **remind the marketer that they themselves may not reflect the consumer** who buys their products. Listening directly to this consumer helps bring the real consumer to life in the minds of marketers.

I usually use a hidden camera for recording these interviews. The participant is fully aware of the recording, but it is not obvious to other shoppers or store personnel that this is anything other than a couple of people out shopping together.

During these trips, I recommend a maximum of one client observer join the shopping trip. This helps maintain the ruse of it being a normal shopping trip for the participant and the retailer. Retailers have been known to ask researchers to leave their stores, which would be a waste of all the preparation efforts, so I try to keep it casual and fly under the radar.

In one project I went shopping one-on-one with women who scrapbook. This consisted of a pre-shop interview (done at a nearby coffee shop) and then going to the adhesives aisle at an arts and crafts supplies retailer to see how each woman reacted to the adhesives products, packaging and merchandising. It was interesting to see the women try to make sense of all the choices on the shelf. Clearly there was an opportunity to use package design to better differentiate the products from one another.

We learned that there are so many different types of craft adhesives, having pictures of the product-in-use on the package was very helpful to guide the crafters to which adhesive would work best for her project. Before this, I had no idea you could use glue spots to

Qualitative Research Methodologies:

adhere embellishments like bows or sequins to a greeting card or scrapbook. Then there are glue pens, glue tape, glue spots with a roll-on applicator, glue spots on paper, adhesive squares, you name it!

I love finding out about whole new worlds I never knew existed through my research experiences. It also helps the brand managers get some perspective on how familiar (or not) various consumers are with their products, which helps marketers design marketing communications that best meet the consumers' needs.

Individual Depth Interviews (IDIs) are one-on-one in-depth interviews about a particular topic. These allow the interviewer to follow an individual's train of thought with probing questions to get to the root of what he or she thinks and does.

For one IDI project, I interviewed individual teenage girls about the role online content plays in their makeup shopping. A beauty products brand wanted to understand what types of content the girls interacted with at each stage of exploring and deciding on which makeup products to buy. These interviews were conducted at a focus group facility to be observed by the client from behind a mirror.

Online—Any of the techniques above can be done online. Doing qualitative research online avoids travel for client and respondents, which can be particularly useful if the participants are spread across a large geographic area or would be hard to get together "live" for any reason, for example, high-level professionals or people with an uncommon disease.

To name just a couple online options, in lieu of focus groups, there are online bulletin boards. Instead of live one-on-ones, interviews can be conducted on the phone or via webcam. Mobile research tools also exist and are being further developed to provide an exciting new way to gain immediate feedback from consumers in the moment of usage or purchase decision.

The landscape of mobile and online research is constantly evolving and I won't go into much depth on them in this book since the information will be quickly outdated.

Qualitative Research, in summary, allows for impromptu probes to dig further into rich lines of questioning. It is best used for understanding consumers' perceptions, opinions, beliefs and attitudes on a given topic to refine ideas for further research or development.

Part Two

The Brand Marketer's Guide to The 5 Stages of Focus Group Research

This guide will help you become a savvier focus group services buyer or conduct your own focus groups. The entire process will take roughly six to eight weeks once you know what you want to learn and have stimuli such as concepts, prototypes or ads ready to show consumers.

The guide has been written with the focus group client in mind. The client could be anyone with an interest in learning the opinions of respondents. They will often be a brand or marketing manager, market research manager, or ad agency strategy/account person, but there are many other possibilities too.

If you have budgeted to work with a focus group moderator or qualitative research consultant, this is the right time to get in touch with them to confirm their availability and begin to discuss the upcoming research project.

The Brand Marketer's Guide to the 5 Stages of Focus Group Research –

STAGE 1: Write the Research Brief
STAGE 2: Recruit the Participants
STAGE 3: Develop the Discussion Guide and Stimuli
STAGE 4: Conduct the Research
STAGE 5: Analyze and Share the Research Results

STAGE 1:
Write The Research Brief

The research brief is the planning document that summarizes the business situation and defines the objectives of your research. It will also lay out the methodology, timeline and costs of the project. Taking time to think through and articulate the objectives and scope of your research will provide a valuable document that you will refer back to often in your research project. **Think of the research brief as the blueprint you will use as you build your project.**

The following process is what I do for each of my clients when they come to me with research objectives. In the beginning, there are usually not formal "research objectives". The client, alone or in collaboration with the research provider, will develop a list of key questions or hypotheses they want to test on a given topic with a specified group of people. Articulating the more formal research objectives will happen subsequently as a part of writing the research brief. The magic question that will help concentrate the research objectives into a cohesive, prioritized list is: **"What decisions will be made based on the learning from this research?"**

Benefits of a Research Brief

The research brief will manage expectations between the marketing research consultant and the client, while also giving the client a document laying out the entire project so it is easy to communicate with senior management. It will also identify what resources to reserve in advance, such as the focus group facility and moderator.

A research brief will get all the stakeholders on the same page from the beginning of the project. A six to eight week research project timeline is based on all interested parties being on the same page regarding what the research will strive to accomplish.

The brief will also improve the utility of the research by defining and refining the project objectives so the learnings from the research are immediately able to help make better-informed business decisions.

How to Write a Research Brief

Typically the marketing research consultant and the client will have a quick phone call to discuss the overall project background and objectives, then the marketing research consultant will use that information to write the research brief. It will be revised and finalized based on further discussions, a process that usually takes about a week, as long as all parties are available to stay in communication. Clients invariably have many projects going on and the research consultant will be expected to follow up and make it as easy as possible for clients to provide feedback.

At this stage the client may want to enter into a nondisclosure agreement (NDA) with the research consultant to protect the client's intellectual property. An NDA can provide legal recourse if a consultant were to, for example, disclose confidential information to a competitive company. In my practice I'm happy to sign them since I would never think of compromising a client's information, but I also don't bring it up if the client doesn't make the request.

While writing the brief, the researcher will get in contact with focus group facilities to obtain availability and bids for reserving a focus suite, recruiting participants, and paying incentives. The costs reflected in my research briefs typically cover all charges except travel and client food at the facilities.

STAGE 1: Write The Research Brief

When done well, **the research brief will be a succinct executive summary of the focus group research plan**. It should be understood and approved by all key stakeholders before the detailed work of focus group planning begins.

The research brief includes 5 sections: Background, Objectives, Methodology, Timeline, and Costs.

1. Background

The background should include the overall state of the business, any relevant market forces—such as competition or consumer trends—and the general purpose for the client's focus group research. It can be provided by the client or drafted by the research consultant based on initial project communications.

Included in the background will be information that is critical for the research consultant to understand. The background should be succinct and be kept to the highlights. Supplementary background materials can be supplied to the consultant once the project has been approved.

2. Objectives

Like the background, the objectives section should be concise and can be provided by the client or drafted by the research consultant for the client's input and approval.

The objectives section should include the primary research objective and a couple secondary research objectives clarifying the content areas for the focus groups.

The section should also include a statement of how the results of the research will be used. Be sure the answer to this question is included: "What decisions will be made based on the learning from this research?" The act of answering and gaining stakeholder agreement to the answer of this question will bring a world of clarity and single-mindedness to the research, which in turn will make the research much more actionable for the business.

Which research methodology should be chosen is dependent on what is the objective of the research. In this book we're talking about focus groups, which are appropriate when the business objective is to understand consumers thoughts about a particular topic in order to gain directional feedback for further development.

Gaining broad support early with all the interested parties, like various functions and levels of management, will help pave the way for prompt action when the research is complete. **It is worthwhile to take the time at this stage to gain agreement on what the research needs to uncover and how the learning will be used.**

3. Methodology

The methodology is often decided in a conversation between the client and research consultant who drafts the methodology section of the research brief.

The methodology should include the dates, times and location of research; a description of the type of respondents required; the group size or the number of participants expected in each focus group; and a description of any homework assignment (optional).

Clients often ask me for guidance on how many focus groups to conduct. The more you do on any one topic, the more confident you can be that the consumer feedback is consistent with a broader population. For instance, if there are differences in attitudes on the topic between geographic areas, you may want to conduct focus groups in more than one market.

STAGE 1: Write The Research Brief

Of course, more groups will cost more money, so it's a balancing act between the level of risk an organization is willing to take and the amount of money it's willing to spend. **At a minimum, I recommend two to three focus groups on any topic with each segment of the target consumer.**

For example, when researching DIY store customers who buy blowtorches, it is a good idea to have at least two groups for each target consumer segment, such as plumbers, chefs and homeowners. They each use the blowtorches for different projects in different environments and therefore have different needs and opinions about the products.

Much like a data point on a chart, it's helpful to have more than one point in order to establish a trend line or a least have some perspective on whether that data point is typical or an outlier.

Making the detailed methodology specification choices is fairly complex, but they can be accomplished quickly with an experienced research professional. Below are the things to keep in mind for deciding the methodology details. The information here is rigorous and important to get right.

a) Dates, times and location of research

- When planning the **dates of the research**, allow enough time to prepare, including two to three weeks for recruiting participants and time for the client to prepare any research stimuli—such as new product concepts, packaging mock-ups or advertising storyboards. Giving a facility less than two weeks to recruit good participants will make it much harder for them to complete a successful recruit.

- Keep holidays and the client observers' availability in mind. Also, be mindful of any local events taking place on the date of your research.

- I have found that I can achieve a higher rate of recruited participants who show up to the research if the focus groups are held on Tuesdays, Wednesdays and Thursdays. More things seem to pop up that prevent recruits from participating on Mondays and Fridays. Conducting research Tuesday through Thursday also leaves Monday and Friday open for travel to and from the research market.

- The subject of the focus group has to be taken into account as well when determining the research schedule. Some subjects lend themselves best to a particular day of the week or time of day. For example, taste-testing new garlic bread flavors at 8 a.m. may not be the best idea, but scheduling those groups around lunch, dinner or snack time would work well.

Time-of-day considerations for ease of recruiting and better show rates:

- Avoid starting groups during morning or afternoon rush hour. Facility staff can provide guidance on traffic near their location.

- If you are recruiting mothers, be aware of school start and end times in the area. Even if you are recruiting mothers of infants, many times those infants will have school-age siblings.

- For many professionals, evening groups are easier to recruit. The lunch hour can also work well; in which case you may want to plan on feeding the participants so their hungry stomachs don't distract them from your topic.

- Many professions now have more flexible hours and daytime groups are not as hard to recruit for as they once were. If you're doing research in the client's home market, they often appreciate conducting groups during the day if possible so they can get home at a reasonable hour.

The **length of the focus group** depends on the amount of material you want to cover and the expected attention span of the respondents. Two-hour groups are fairly typical. That will allow for enough time to warm up the respondents, have a general discussion about the topic, then have time for two to three sections of in-depth discussion and leave a few minutes at the end for any questions from the client observers.

The **amount of time to leave between groups** is important too. You must give the moderator enough time to clear the room and set up for the next group, without leaving so much time in between that the client observers feel like their time is being wasted. I like a minimum of half an hour or an hour if the client would like to do a mini-debrief between each group. More time can be left in between groups if you plan on refining the stimuli between groups. For example, you may have written new product concept statements that you would like to refine after getting feedback from each group.

Location, location, location…

The primary location consideration in choosing the location for research is **determining which market(s)** are representative of the population you want to talk with. Make sure people living in the area are familiar with or use the product categories or brands you want to discuss. Be cognizant of where the headquarters of brands are located, because being in a company's hometown can lead to bias in the groups that may have more to do with that company as an employer than the company's products or services.

The second part of location is **determining which focus group facilities** to use. Personal experience or referrals from others who have used a specific facility are the best sources of information.

Impulse Survey is a research industry source where the focus group moderators rate each facility they use overall and on a number of variables. Look at how many moderators have contributed to a facility's ratings to judge how trustworthy the rating is. Another good indicator is how many years a facility has held a good rating, since the survey is updated annually.

There are other directories such as GreenBook and Blue Book. They are in business to drive ad sales from research facilities—I am usually able to find the information just as easily through an online search.

At this point you have already made many focus group planning decisions and you are about half way done with the research brief. Take a quick restorative break and come back with a fresh mind. Rest assured, this detailed planning up front will pay off win a smooth, well-run research project.

b)   Description of the type of respondents required

As I have mentioned, I recommend conducting **at least two focus groups with any one type of respondent**. Having more than one set of data from a given respondent segment will allow you to compare and contrast between groups. It will also help establish trends and identify outliers in responses.

The specific make-up of the groups can be determined later in the research process when the participant screener has been written. **What is most important to decide at this stage is the number of total groups and the number of research days**, which is the information you will need to reserve focus group facility space.

STAGE 1: Write The Research Brief

Product users, competitive product users, brand loyalists, age segments (E.g. 18-22, 23-30, 31-40, 41+), genders, education, employment, sizes of family, and type of dwelling, etc. are examples of aspects you may use to define your target respondents.

Whether or not ages and genders should be mixed will depend on the topic of the group. Usually, the more sensitive the topic, the more homogenous the group will need to be in order to empower everyone to talk freely (E.g. female incontinence products). On the other hand, sometimes it helps to mix up the groups in order to minimize groupthink. For example, a group of all male financial planners ages 25-40 may conform to each other's answers and be less interesting than a wider mix of ages and genders.

c)   Group size

Individual group size, multiplied by the number of groups, determines the total number of participants in the study. "Group size" on the Research Brief will indicate how large each individual focus group will be, including the number of respondents being recruited and seated for each group.

Bigger is not necessarily better. I have found that eight respondents is the maximum effective number for most of the groups I do. Any more than that can lead to superficial answers and limit the amount of material that can be covered. Smaller groups of two to four people are excellent for gaining more in-depth detail and consumer language on a particular topic.

Research participants do not all show up to their scheduled research. They are human and extenuating circumstances do happen. For example: bad traffic, forgetting, having to stay home with sick kids, urgent business or professional matters, etc. To ensure full groups, recruit more people than actually needed. I often recruit eight to seat six to eight, or I recruit six to seat four to six. This will incur additional recruiting and incentive fees for the extra respondents, but chances are good that not everyone will show up. Incentives are only paid to respondents who show up. To me, over-recruiting is worthwhile insurance against not having enough respondents show.

d) Homework assignment (optional)

Homework is often assigned to get the participant thinking about the topic ahead of time. There is usually an additional incentive paid to the participant and an additional administrative fee paid to the recruiter for managing the homework.

I have found that for niche product conversations, it is very useful to have participants send in pictures of the specific products to be discussed ahead of time. This will ensure the participants are familiar with the exact product. For example, one time I did focus groups about rear engine riding lawn mowers. Many people did not seem to catch the words <u>rear engine</u> and we had to turn away several regular tractor-type (forward engine) riding lawn mower owners. To be honest, I had never even heard of a rear engine riding lawn mower before that project, so I could understand the consumers' confusion.

Since those groups, whenever I have any doubt that people understand exactly which product we are talking about, I have them send in pictures. Product confusion is more prevalent than most manufacturers expect. In the past, I have needed respondents who've used foam board rather than just regular poster board, homeowners who have needed to have used fertilizer with crabgrass preventer instead of the more common fertilizer with weed killer, people with permanently installed standby electric generators versus just anybody with a back-up generator. You get the idea.

STAGE 1: Write The Research Brief

Homework, more broadly, is an easy way to get more information from the same participants when it is hard to cover everything within the time of the focus group itself. Make it simple though. It can be intimidating and overwhelming if the homework is too involved.

4. Timeline

Develop a timeline that identifies the tasks, person responsible and due date for each task. Assuming the creative stimuli for the research is not a time constraint, a typical qualitative consumer insights project will take roughly six to eight weeks. Below is an achievable timeline, when the research itself can be completed within one week. You may need more time if you are covering multiple geographic areas.

Week 1: Develop and gain approval for research brief

Week 2: Write and gain approval for participant screener. Start recruiting.

Week 3: Continue recruiting. Develop the discussion guide outline.

Week 4: Continue recruiting. Develop and finalize the detailed discussion guide and any necessary research stimuli.

Week 5: Conduct research.

Week 6: Publish the quick summary report in document form.

Week 7: Submit final detailed report in presentation format.

5. Costs

There are so many different variables in the cost of qualitative market research that it is hard to pin down an "average" cost.

That said, when you are new to it, an order-of-magnitude idea of how much these studies cost is exactly what people crave, so I am going to give you a *rough* cost estimate. You've got all of those caveats, right?

At the time of this writing a two-day round of six focus groups (three per day) with six participants each in one geographical market will cost around $30,000 to $40,000, excluding travel costs. That covers the cost of the focus group moderator, planning, conducting and reporting on the research. It also includes the cost of the focus suite space, reception and hosting, plus the cost of recruiting and paying incentives to the participants.

Of course, you will know the potential upside opportunity and downside risk in your business better than I would, so you can be the judge of what focus groups are worth to you. If focus groups save the business from spending $500,000 to produce a marketing campaign that is going to offend consumers and hurt the popularity of your brand, then $30,000 to $40,000 sounds like a good value. If your business is going to spend hundreds of thousands of dollars to build the equipment that will make a product, it's probably a good idea to hear confirmation from consumers that this product meets their expectations and if not, what you can do to improve it.

If you're running a regional or smaller business, $30,000 to $40,000 might not be a reasonable budget for you. In that case you will need to get creative about talking with consumers, possibly without the assistance of an experienced market research consultant. You can do it. It just takes more time and effort on your part.

I have done pro bono projects for non-profit organizations for much lower costs, but a lot of improvising takes place to make that happen. For instance, the focus groups can be conducted onsite at the organization's headquarters with participants from a contact list the organization already has. This has its drawbacks; such as the introduction of bias by talking only to people the organization already knows. Participants may also feel more intimidated to speak freely in front of someone they know has a vested interest in the outcome of the research.

Again, there are too many variables in the cost of qualitative market research to pin down a true average cost. Costs are influenced by myriad things: the number of participants you speak to, who those participants are, which and how many geographies you cover, and whether or not you ask the participants to complete any homework before the day of the research.

If you write the rest of the research brief first with a rough budget in mind, then the client and research consultant can collaborate to refine the study design, making sure it meets the most important learning objectives within the timing and cost requirements.

Summary - Write the Research Brief

It's true that writing the research brief can be dry, tedious work. For those of us who love to plan though, this is an interesting part of the project that requires experience and creativity, and provides an opportunity for enjoyable, open communication between the research consultant and the client.

Nailing down a detailed research brief will make the rest of the process go more smoothly. The research objectives pave the way for the participant recruiting screener survey, the discussion guide and ultimately the research results. The research brief will truly be the foundation of your research project.

Stage 2:
Recruit The Participants

The Brand Marketer's Guide to the 5 Stages of Focus Group Research –
STAGE 1: Write the Research Brief
STAGE 2: Recruit the Participants
STAGE 3: Develop the Discussion Guide and Stimuli
STAGE 4: Conduct the Research
STAGE 5: Analyze and Share the Research Results

Recruiting the right participants is an incredibly important part of any consumer insights project, because only the thoughts and actions of the *relevant target audience* will impact the business.

Image created by jscreationzs. www.freedigitalphotos.net

Stage 2: Recruit The Participants

Talking to the wrong people is a waste of time. And embarrassing. You do not want to be the brand manager in charge when the vice president of marketing asks why you didn't make sure these people were the ones who actually *use* the product—as opposed to just the people responsible for picking up what their spouse ask them to get at the store.

If a non-qualified participant makes it into your study, it becomes a waste of the recruiting and incentive cost of that respondent, which is likely $200-300 all together. It can also make the dynamic of a focus group a bit awkward if the moderator has to excuse a participant during the group when it becomes apparent they do not qualify.

To get the right respondents, I write a thorough screener survey. Even still, I've had to excuse a few participants during the groups over the years. Each time it happens I learn something new and update my screener accordingly.

For instance, I do quite a bit of work in my home market of Columbus, Ohio. In one of my focus groups a woman arrived who I had done a shop-along interview with a few months before. This was not ideal because I did not want her familiarity with me to bias her answers or change the dynamic of the group. I excused her and she was still paid the incentive for showing up. However, now on my screeners in Columbus, I ask the focus group facility to check their database to make sure the respondents have not participated in any research with me previously.

Seven Steps to Recruiting Top-Notch Participants

Recruiting participants for research involves multiple steps. Be clear and specific about the people you want to gain feedback from in your research, and give the recruiter enough time to find them. **A good rule of thumb is having the screener survey done <u>three weeks</u> before the focus groups begin.**

Here are the seven steps for recruiting participants:

1. The client and market researcher **identify the detailed specifications each of the respondents should meet.**

   For general requirements I typically ask gender, age, marital status, ethnicity, employment, education and income. I also include questions to make sure they speak English clearly, articulate well, are willing to state their opinions and are open to thinking about new ideas.

   I use a security-screening question to rule out anyone who is in a profession that we would not want to talk with, such as someone from an advertising agency, market research firm, media outlet, or someone who works in a company that makes or sells the type of product or service we will be discussing. I usually also add a requirement that they have not done any research in the past six months and that they have never done research on the topic of these focus groups.

   The unique specifications vary with each research study. They can include things such as number and age of household members, type of dwelling, brand awareness, someone who is not a rejecter of purchasing a particular brand in the future, someone who bought a particular product or service in a specified time frame, or used that product or service recently or is considering purchasing a product or service in a certain amount of time.

   A friend who works in Mexico City reminded me of the importance of understanding the culture of the respondents too. For instance, in Mexico when one person states their opinion, the rest of the people in the group are more likely to go along with that opinion rather than create conflict.

   Dominant participants, if not managed well, can have ill effects in any country, but in Mexico, group harmony is a particularly

Stage 2: Recruit The Participants

strong value. Researchers have to be cognizant of, and adjust for, the cultural anomalies of whatever market they're operating in. There will be many similarities, but also many differences to be aware of when conducting qualitative research in various U.S. states, let alone other countries.

2. The market researcher will **write a questionnaire for the recruiters to use to find people who qualify for the study.** Depending on the complexity of the screener survey and the amount of involvement from the client, writing the survey can take about a week from start to final, approved document, including a draft and revision in between. As a point of reference, my screeners tend to be 20-25 questions long. Shorter is better because you don't want to lose potential participants to survey fatigue.

   At this stage you must have a final research schedule so the recruiters have date and time slots to fill with qualified participants. See the **Writing the Research Brief** section of this book for tips on planning the research schedule.

3. The recruiter will **send an email blast out to people in their database who meet the broad specifications for the study.** The email should ask if they would be willing to take a quick phone survey to see if they qualify for paid market research. The email blast will not give away the contents of the study and the screener survey itself should not be posted online where a respondent could see all the questions at the same time. These are safeguards that high quality recruiters will have in place so that you get fresh, qualified participants for your study.

4. The recruiters will **call the consumers that respond to the email with interest in participating in the study**, in a process sometimes affectionately referred to as "smiling and dialing." They will ask the questions from the screener survey until the consumer

has a disqualifying answer, at which point the consumer will be thanked and told they do not qualify for this particular study. Many products have 10% incidence levels or less (meaning less than 10% of the population buys the product). This means a lot of thanking and ending will take place before the recruiters find enough qualified people to participate in the research.

Here's a hypothetical example of "incidence level." Everyone uses toothpaste (100% incidence), but a smaller percentage uses toothpaste for sensitive teeth (maybe 30%). An even smaller percentage uses sensitive toothpaste with extra whitening power (possibly 5-10%). The particular study in question might only be interested in talking with sensitive, whitening toothpaste users who are open (or at least do not object) to trying a particular toothpaste brand. You can see how the incidence levels can get low quickly. This is why recruiting the right consumers takes more time and money than you might expect.

When recruiters reach a consumer who qualifies for the study (i.e. makes it through the entire screener survey), they will schedule the respondent for a focus group.

5. The recruiters **will give verbal instructions and follow that up with written confirmation that has the date, time, and location of the research.** The confirmation will also include the amount of incentive the participant will be paid, driving directions, and homework instructions. Respondents will then be requested to show up fifteen minutes before the start of the group for check-in so the research is sure to start on time. The day before the research, recruiters will call the scheduled respondents to re-confirm their participation.

Be sure to **set the incentive** high enough to make it worthwhile for respondents. This might be $100+ for two-hour groups depending on the type of participants needed. For something

Stage 2: Recruit The Participants

quicker, like a ninety-minute group, the incentive can be lower, around $75 for an average household products consumer at the time of this writing.

When you want to talk to professionals, such as doctors, the incentive can easily be twice these rates or more. The recruiter will have a recommendation for what the rate needs to be set at to incentivize participants from your target market in the geographic area.

6. When the first participants start being scheduled, the recruiter **shares a daily profile of the scheduled respondents** with the market researcher. The recruiter prepares a profile spreadsheet of the respondents, with a tab for each group time. Each tab in the spreadsheet has the participants' names and screener answers to give the client and research consultant an overview of who is participating.

7. Finally, **adjustments to the screener may have to be made during the recruiting process**. The recruiter will call attention to any qualifications they are having a hard time finding people to meet. What often happens is that the recruiter will place respondents on "hold" if they nearly qualify for the study but are off by one specification. If the recruiter has a hard time filling the study with participants, the client and research consultant will review the holds and decide whether some compromises can be made to accept a few more respondents. For example, the screener may have been written with the requirement that the minimum household income of respondents had to be above $45,000, but if the consumer qualifies on every other specification this one may not be as important.

The research consultant will check the participant profile updates daily and let the client know how the recruiting is going. If there are any recruiting difficulties, these should be recognized and addressed as early as possible to give the recruiter time to react and get the study filled.

Don't make the mistake of compromising the quality of your recruiting process to get the research project done more quickly. Instead, plan ahead to leave room in the schedule for consumer research and direct management's expectations of when the very useful consumer feedback will be available.

Summary—Recruit the Participants

As you can see from this chapter, recruiting the research participants is important, complex and can get fairly technical. You want someone who will pay close attention to the details to manage this part of the project. This is probably not the most "fun" part of consumer insights work, but it is critical to making sure you have the right people in your focus groups.

Recruiting participants is a part of the research project that is definitely worth outsourcing. A great professional recruiter can be hired to take care of all of these details. Many focus groups facilities have in-house recruiting services. Professional recruiters have the databases and the expertise to get qualified respondents for research.

For a great guide to writing the participant screener questionnaire, refer to *The Complete Guide to Writing Questionnaires* written by David F. Harris.

STAGE 3:
Develop The Discussion Guide and Stimuli

It takes thoughtful planning and creativity to develop a discussion guide that will get the most insightful answers on your research objectives in the time allotted.

The Brand Marketer's Guide to the 5 Stages of Focus Group Research –
STAGE 1: Write the Research Brief
STAGE 2: Recruit the Participants
STAGE 3: Develop the Discussion Guide and Stimuli
STAGE 4: Conduct the Research
STAGE 5: Analyze and Share the Research Results

At its core, the **discussion guide is a set of agreed upon questions for the respondents**. Think of the discussion guide as the set of steps the moderator will follow.

The **stimuli** are whatever will be presented to participants to prompt discussion. This will be unique to each business. Stimuli could be new product concepts, advertising storyboards, package designs—the possibilities are endless. Stimuli are mentioned at this stage because they must be complete before the research is conducted.

Benefits of a qualitative research discussion guide

The key benefits of having a discussion guide are:

1. Knowing the moderator and client are in sync on what to expect.
2. Establishing priorities and time parameters on each topic for the moderator.
3. Making sure there are an optimal number and type of activities to keep respondents engaged throughout the discussion.
4. Establishing the flow so that early topics do not bias subjects to be talked about later in the discussion.
5. Phrasing the questions ahead of time to ensure they are clear and will bring out the information you need, without "leading" the participants toward any particular response.

How to create a discussion guide for qualitative research

Four things to keep in mind when creating a discussion guide for qualitative research:

1. The research objectives
2. Who you will be talking with
3. The amount of time you have in each session
4. The environment (i.e. focus group room, retail store, home, etc.)

Start with a discussion outline

Before writing the detailed discussion guide, the market research consultant or moderator will sketch out a discussion outline for feedback from the client to make sure they're on the same page in terms of priorities, flow and timing. It's a lot easier to move and change things in an outline than it is once you get into the detailed language of the full discussion guide. **The discussion outline is an ordered list of discussion topics, along with a purpose and time allotment for each topic.**

When forwarding the discussion outline to a client for feedback, I include a copy of the Research Brief so they have the objectives, participant specifications and research timeline right there for reference.

Writing the discussion guide

The discussion guide will typically begin with 10-15 minutes of introductions, participant guidelines and warm up. The amount of time needed will depend on the number of people in the discussion. Then you will get into the general topic and transition to more specific topics as everyone talks comfortably and is well established in speaking their minds.

Three guiding principles for developing any research discussion guide are:

1. Start broad and then get more specific

2. Use short questions to get open, in-depth answers

3. Express inquiries so they are not biased toward a certain response

It's easiest to establish a rapport within a group while seated at the table, and then have a variety of discussion techniques and activities to keep everyone engaged as the session progresses.

Several things will need to be accomplished in the introductions:

- Explain the **independent, unbiased role of the moderator** as the person who will direct the session to get the needed feedback in the allotted time. Let them know there are no wrong answers. The moderator just needs to understand what the respondents think, do and feel. The moderator did not come up with any of the ideas being presented for feedback.

- Tell the respondents if and how they are being recorded, whether it's **audio or video recording** or both. I tell them they are being recorded so I can refer back to the recordings to help me summarize the findings in my report. I often say they won't be getting famous on YouTube from our research, which usually get a laugh from the group and helps break the tension.

- Let the respondents know that the moderator has **colleagues behind the mirror** who are interested in hearing what the respondents have to say. I often say that it would be too crowded and too distracting to have everyone in the room, then I wave to the folks behind the mirror and the participants barely remember they're there the rest of the time.

- Let the respondents know that the moderator needs to **hear from everyone roughly equally**, that each of the participants was specially recruited to represent a segment of the population outside the research, and that the moderator will be guiding the discussion to make sure everyone is heard. Tell them it's okay if they do not agree on everything. Everyone's unique viewpoint is valuable and hearing a differing opinion can help others clarify their own point of view.

- Tell the participants that the group is on a first name only basis and their **privacy is being protected** in that way.

STAGE 3: Develop The Discussion Guide and Stimuli

Considerations for the core content of the discussion guide

So let's say the moderator is working on a discussion guide for a typical two-hour focus group. The first fifteen minutes is **introductions and warm-up**, so they have an hour and forty-five minutes left. That may sound like a lot, but I find the time flies and it helps to have everything mapped out ahead of time.

After the introductions the next section is very likely going to be spent getting information on participants' **attitudes and usage of the relevant product category**. For instance, when I spoke with hunters and fishing enthusiasts about a potential new mobile app, first I needed to understand what kind of hunting or fishing they did and whether or not they brought their smartphone along with them during their outdoor activities.

I like to **switch activities every 20-30 minutes** or so. That gives me the opportunity to change the dynamic in the room and look at the topic from a new angle, which can help get deeper feedback from more participants. Just like different students learn better through different teaching methods, **different research participants respond better to different research activities**.

When switching activities I try to think about the activities' effects on the energy in the room. If participants have been sitting and calling out feedback to the moderator in free association, which is fairly passive for respondents, I might make the next activity something they need to do with their hands or get out of their seat to do.

A good practice is to **keep the activity instructions as simple as possible**. You don't want the moderator using a lot of research time to explain what the participants need to do. Also, you don't want the participants to be so distracted by following intricate instructions that their minds can't focus on the actual topic. For each activity, instructions need to be given and they need to be easy to understand.

To minimize "group think" I like having participants jot down their thoughts independently before we begin any group discussion.

For example, I might ask them to read through a new product description, highlight or circle what they like, cross through what they don't like and give it a rating of one to five (or a grade of A-F) on how much the product idea appeals to them. Then I stand at the easel and go around the table, while everyone calls out their ratings to me before we plunge into what they liked and didn't like about the product idea. This process gives the respondents a chance to crystallize their own thinking before anyone else in the room says something that may sway their opinion.

Go-to activities for focus groups

There are no official rules for how exactly to guide the discussion topics. A core competency of good moderators is using their creativity when coming up with focus group activities. The activities need to fit with the style of the moderator, respondents and client observers. Below are a few of the methods I often use and customize for each client's particular needs.

Free Association—when the moderator asks respondents to call out words, images or feelings that come to mind regarding a particular topic. I often like to use this as an exercise to understand how brands are regarded and to understand the differences perceived between various brands.

For example, in groups about bicycles, I could start with Huffy, Schwinn or Trek and have participants call out what comes to mind for each brand. Once there's an easel page list for each brand, the unique essence of each brand starts to become apparent. After the groups, it's interesting to see the differences in brand perceptions between the various groups of people in the study.

Likes/Dislikes or Pro/Con lists—This is a good, simple exercise to do with the moderator at the easel board as the group calls out

STAGE 3: Develop The Discussion Guide and Stimuli

what comes to mind. It's basically a more organized version of free association. I like to use this method to identify features and benefits to highlight in marketing messages and areas of opportunity for further development.

Even when a business team thinks they know the good, bad and ugly about their product, it can be enlightening to hear it from the consumers' perspective. This is particularly true when you are talking with a specific segment of consumers that you don't know as well. (E.g. Hispanics, Baby Boomers, Millennials, etc.)

Sorts—a technique in which participants are given a number of things to categorize or put in order. A sort can help a business team understand the broader context in which their brand exists.

Examples of sorting exercises:

To help a client understand where their brand falls in the consumers' minds: The moderator can have brand logos printed out and ask the participants to work as a team, sorting them from most premium to least premium. A spokesperson for the group will then tells the moderator how they decided where to put each brand. Majority rules for the sort on the table, but dissenters are encouraged to say why they feel a brand belongs in a different order. The logos can be sorted on any relevant criteria—from most traditional to most innovative, most expensive to least expensive, highest quality to lowest quality—whatever it is the business needs to learn the most about.

To help a business understand specifically what products they may be competing against, the moderator can have participants sort product packages into groups representing which products they would consider together. This activity can help illustrate the segments within a given category. For example with soup, if I put a bunch of packages of soup on the table, respondents might sort them into cooking soups, eating soups, stews, lighter soups, vegetarian soups, canned soups, soup in pouches, etc.

Here's a real-life example of a ten-minute sort exercise used in focus groups on convenience store brands. In these groups, the client and their advertising agency were looking for insights on what brand messages would resonate most with frequent convenience store shoppers.

This exercise was intended to help confirm the brand's core competitive brands. The immediate result of the exercise was a conference table full of convenience store brand logos sorted into clusters such as truck stops, daily morning stop (for gas and coffee), specialty, etc. and a robust discussion of the players within the various clusters.

Comparing the results from multiple groups gave the client a good basis of understanding and perspective to start their creative messaging ideation. The following are the actual instructions pulled from the discussion guide:

1. *C-STORE SORT EXERCISE: Now, I would like you to work as a team to sort a few convenience store logos into groups where you think the brands relate in some way and label each group.*

2. *Debrief with the group of respondents.*

   - *What do the brands grouped together have in common? What did you label them?*

   - *What's different about the various brand groups?*

   - *Who do the various brand groups appeal to?*

   - *In what ways are they shopped differently?*

   New Product Concept Feedback—The key here is to start with a simple description of the new product or service, written to the audience that will make the purchase, including what benefits it offers and why those benefits are superior to other choices the consumer has.

STAGE 3: Develop The Discussion Guide and Stimuli

Most marketers are way too close to their products, services and brands to see them clearly from a consumer perspective. It helps immensely to **use a clear product concept to boil down the essence of what is uniquely being offered** to whom and for what reasons this offering is superior to other choices. With a clear concept, consumers are reacting to the heart of the idea and not led astray by extraneous information.

Anyone who has worked with Procter & Gamble in marketing has learned their insight, benefit, and reason-to-believe method for crafting concepts. In a nutshell a good concept for gaining consumer reaction is constructed like this example:

<u>Concept Title</u>: *New NutraJuice!*

<u>Insight</u>: *As a Mom, it's a battle to get my children to take in enough nutrition from fruits and vegetables.*

<u>Benefit</u>: *NutraJuice gives the fruit and vegetable nutrition Moms want in a delicious, fruity drink kids will love!*

<u>Reason-to-believe</u>: *That's because, NutraJuice has the sweet juice flavors kids enjoy. It's made with real fruits and vegetables, and provides 100% of the daily-recommended allowance of vitamins A and C.*

<u>Closing</u>: *Give your kids NutraJuice. With the delicious, fruity taste kids love, and the fruit and vegetable nutrition they need, everybody wins!*

Of course, the final version the focus group participants will see does not include the section labels like the example above. **Concept writing is an important skill for brand marketers** and it's worth investing time to learn to do it well. From a research perspective, the concepts need to have a single-minded benefit, <u>be simple enough for the consumers to understand quickly</u>, and be obviously different from each other if you want them to compare concepts to each other.

Concept writing <u>mistakes</u> marketers often make for research are:

- Including <u>too many benefits</u> or reasons-to-believe in each concept, which makes it hard to understand specifically what the consumers are reacting to.

- Writing in <u>technical terms</u> instead of regular consumer language, which makes the concept less relevant to the consumer.

- <u>Making the concepts too similar</u> to each other. Brand managers are typically too close to the business to judge whether concepts are differentiated. It's a good idea to have someone else provide feedback before the research to ensure consumers will be able to easily tell the ideas apart.

For step-by-step instructions on clear concept writing, read <u>Marketing Concepts That Win!</u> by Martha Guidry. I've referred back to that book many times over the years when I have needed to write concepts.

Once the client has written a great concept, or a few unique ones to compare, here's what the moderator does:

1. Tell the participants what the process will be. Let them know you will be passing out the concept to everyone and reading it aloud to them while they read along to themselves. Before any discussion begins, ask them to:

   a) Jot their first impressions at the top of the page.

   b) Rate the concept 1-5 (or A, B, C, D, F) based on how much it appeals to them (1 = Very appealing, 2 = Somewhat appealing, 3 = Neither appealing nor unappealing, 4 = Somewhat unappealing, 5 = Very unappealing) and write their rating at the top of the page.

STAGE 3: Develop The Discussion Guide and Stimuli

    c) Highlight or circle words or images that they like and cross through words or images they don't like.

    d) If there is more than one concept to react to—and once all concepts have been read and rated—rank the concepts from most appealing to least appealing.

    **I will post those simple instructions on the wall for reference as well.

2. Pass out the one-page concept to each participant and read it aloud. I find that it's most effective to allow the respondents to read along as I read aloud. This addresses the needs of both visual and audio learners, and ensures that the entire room of people stays at the same pace.

3. Give participants a few minutes to react to and rate the concept individually. Do steps two and three for each concept, and then ask participants to rank the concepts in order of appeal.

4. Go around the table and ask participants to call out their concept ratings and rankings so you can record them on the easel pad. The overall ratings and rankings can give you direction in choosing which concept to discuss first.

5. For each concept, discuss first reactions, likes, dislikes and any other hot button issues there may be for that particular concept. Also ask if the concept is unique, to what extent it is believable and if there are areas consumers would need more information to make a decision. I like to jot down a concept's group feedback on one easel page per concept.

    Package Design Feedback—Focus groups are inherently unrealistic places for consumers to observe packaging designs and predict what actions they would take based on those designs. That said, you could still get very useful feedback to help guide further design development if you structure the conversation thoughtfully, as described below.

First, I like to show the individual package designs in the context of a retail shelf set and find out which packages best catch their eye. **If a package doesn't attract attention on shelf, the copy and design details won't have a chance to sell the product.**

Showing the retail shelf can be done in various ways depending on the space you have available and what resources you have. I've done focus groups where we built actual product shelves and put real live products on it. In other cases, I've brought life sized (or as close to life sized as possible) photos of shelves that were taken at other places. To make the "new" designs seem as lifelike as possible you can tape a new label on the current package form (such as the box or bottle). It also works to digitally substitute the new package for the current package in a photo.

This is an example of questions I asked teens in focus groups about a skincare brand's potential new package design "families." (I'm using design "family" here to mean a design theme that is adapted to various specific products offered by a single brand, such as various design themes that could be carried across individual skincare products, like cream, pads, and face wash.)

Please notice how **it's not just the original question but also the follow up probes that help get the most robust feedback** from respondents.

1. *Which package design family best catches your attention? What about it stands out?*

2. *From which package design family would you be most likely to buy? For what reasons?*

3. *Which package design family makes you feel it would work best for you? What makes you say that?*

4. *Which package design family is most distinctive or unique? How so?*

STAGE 3: Develop The Discussion Guide and Stimuli

5. Which package design family has the highest quality look? <u>Tell me more</u>.

6. Which shelf set would you like to shop at best? <u>Please explain</u>.

7. Which shelf set says best that the brand understands me? <u>In what ways</u>?

Product or Prototype Usage—Focus groups can be used to see firsthand what consumers think of a new product formulation or prototype. The focus group methodology doesn't mimic exactly how the product would be experienced in real life, but there are upsides. Several people from the business team can see the consumer experience "live" and ask new questions in the moment of usage. You can also get feedback from several consumers in a short amount of time.

Respondents can also build off the comments they hear from other participants. **Many times people will notice something but can only articulate their feedback as a reaction to comments they hear from other people**. The moderator has to be careful to look for original feedback and challenge the participants on it if you think they are just piling on to another's feedback, even though it's not a comment that means a great deal to them.

The stimuli, such as products or prototypes, should remain hidden until it is time for that part of the discussion. Keeping the stimuli hidden will help reduce distraction earlier in the group. It also prevents bias that can happen if all the respondents aren't introduced to the stimuli in the same way at the same time. Dark fabric can be draped over the stimuli to "hide" it.

Here's an example of an exercise done with homeowners trying out a new pressure washer model. Thirty minutes was scheduled to do this exercise with eight focus group participants after they had already provided feedback on the product concept. We wanted to see if the product-in-use would live up to the expectations set by the product idea.

In the parking lot behind the focus group facility product engineers had set up two stations where respondents tried using the pressure washer to complete different tasks designed to imitate cleaning situations they might encounter outside their own homes. The prototypes were not branded, and the engineers that facilitated the exercises did not wear logos that showed which company was sponsoring the research.

Here's how it was presented in the focus group: "In this section we get to go outside and each of you will get to try out the new product we've been talking about. We're going to be doing 'test mini-projects' like moving stones or mulch off a sidewalk or cleaning mildew from deck boards."

**Participants are instructed to not discuss anything during this time. Everyone will be given a clipboard with a scoring sheet. When they are waiting their turn, they will <u>not</u> be facing the exercise. After they have had a turn, participants will be filling out a worksheet with their pre- and post-use impressions, likes, dislikes, frustrations, ideas for usage, improvements and post-use purchase interest. After everyone has a chance to try out the product, we will return to the focus room to discuss their impressions.

Advertising Feedback—Sometimes during creative development, agencies would like to get consumer feedback to advertising ideas in a rough stage before they go through the expense of producing the advertising.

Focus groups do not include enough respondents to predict which advertising ideas will do best in market, but they are good for judging what is being communicated to the target audience and for identifying miscommunications that are inexpensive to modify in the idea stage.

Here's an example of a fifteen-minute exercise with a six-person focus group about a potential television advertisement for all-purpose glue:

Note, the creative should be shown to each group in a different

STAGE 3: Develop The Discussion Guide and Stimuli

order to prevent order bias (i.e. always loving or hating the first or last one shown). The ideas should get an equal chance to be shown first, second, third, etc.

The creative should also be described and then read out loud by the moderator. This should be done matter-of-factly, not dramatically. It allows for the respondents to mentally process the creative work both visually and aurally. Plus, it helps keep the participants working at the same pace.

<u>Written Exercise [5 minutes]</u> -

This is our first ad, called _____.

- *Show and read the storyboard (rotate order).*

- *Pass out a feedback sheet with the five questions below to each participant.*

    o *What is your first reaction to this TV ad?*

    o *What main product benefit does the ad communicate to you? Is the benefit believable?*

    o *What do you like about the ad?*

    o *What do you dislike about the ad?*

    o *How likely would you be to purchase this product if you saw this TV ad? From 5 – Definitely would buy, down to 1 – Definitely would not buy*

- *For each storyboard, the moderator will describe the visuals in the scenes, and then will read the copy (narrative) through twice. The moderator will ask the respondents to write the answers before the group discussion begins.*

Group Discussion [10 minutes] -

Ok, let's talk about the ad we've been considering. [The group will then talk about their answers to the questions above to start the discussion. Follow up questions will be asked.]

- *Does this product seem unique? What about the ad makes this product seem unique?*

- *Does this fit with how you think of the brand? How so?*

- *If you saw this ad on TV do you think you would remember it? What makes you say that?*

- *Would you remember the advertised product?*

- *Would you remember the brand name of the product?*

- *Is there any information missing that would be important in helping you choose which glue to buy?*

Collage—One thing I do less frequently in focus groups now is collage. I think a picture can say a thousand words and I like collages for that, but they are time-consuming. Since the minutes I have with my participants are limited, I don't want to spend the time watching respondents sift through magazines and cutting and pasting pictures and words.

If I, or the client, feel a collage would be informative, I like to assign it as homework before the discussion takes place. That way the participants can choose pictures and words from magazines, websites, their own photos, or anywhere else they feel communicates the ideas or feelings they want to express. This way, they spend time choosing and constructing *outside* the focus room and time talking with me *in* the focus room about why they chose what they did.

STAGE 3: *Develop The Discussion Guide and Stimuli*

Final Thoughts on the Discussion Guide

No matter how thoroughly the client and consultant have thought through the discussion guide, plan on opportunistically following interesting lines of discussion that are not in the guide and making modifications to the guide after the first focus group. Sometimes, changes needed are not obvious until you have heard real consumers respond to a topic.

To recap, it's important to have a discussion guide because you do not want to waste the precious minutes you have with these specially selected research participants. Two hours will fly by. You want to have thought through what you want to get out of the session and how the discussion will flow.

For a complete guide to focus group activity options, read *Moderating to the Max* by Jean Bystedt, Siri Lynn and Deborah Potts, Ph.D. Whenever I'm looking for a new focus group activity, I check there first for inspiration.

For still more insights on conducting focus groups from one of the qualitative research industry originals, read *Secrets of a Master Moderator* by Naomi Henderson, CEO of RIVA Market Research and Training Institute.

STAGE 4:
Conduct The Research

Research is a team effort. Everyone involved (moderator, client observers, participants, facility personnel) has an important role in making the research a success.

The Brand Marketer's Guide to the 5 Stages of Focus Group Research –
STAGE 1: Write the Research Brief
STAGE 2: Recruit the Participants
STAGE 3: Develop the Discussion Guide and Stimuli
STAGE 4: Conduct the Research
STAGE 5: Analyze and Share the Research Results

STAGE 4: Conduct The Research

This is the qualitative researcher's version of starring in and producing a theatre production. As a moderator with a background in business management and marketing, conducting the research and applying the learnings to business objectives give me many opportunities to put multiple talents to work.

This chapter will give tips and tricks for the focus group moderator and the client observers. My hope is that it will help you maximize your effectiveness in the research process by giving you the confidence of having knowledge on your side. For me, the knowledge came largely through trial and error over more than a decade of conducting focus groups. I hope this chapter will help save you that time.

The Moderator's Role

The moderator has a lot on her (or his) plate the day of the research. She (or he) is hoping everyone will get there on time. She is helping maintain optimal energy levels for everyone involved. She is setting up materials for the focus room and the backroom. She is managing participant dynamics while covering all the key discussion points and activities within the focus groups on time. And, ultimately, she is making sure the client gets the learnings they need from the research.

When facilitating the focus groups, the moderator's main jobs are:

- Completing the discussion guide fully and on time

- Communicating unconditional positive regard for the participants

- Building temporary personal relationships with respondents

- Drawing out quiet respondents

- Managing assertive or loud respondents

Logistics—They say hope is not a strategy and that is true here. Communicating early and often is the key to getting everyone to the right place at the right time, including the researcher, clients and participants.

For me as the moderator, I make it a policy to stay in the city of the research location the night before research is to begin. I have learned that by trial and error.

> For one study in Milwaukee I was scheduled to fly out of Columbus first thing in the morning for focus groups later that afternoon. There were a few hours between the flight's scheduled arrival and the start of the focus groups so I could manage any potential flight delays. Flights delays would have been ok, but I hadn't planned for a flight cancellation! I didn't find out until I arrived at the Columbus airport at 6 a.m. the day of the research that my flight had been cancelled.
>
> After hurriedly consulting Google Maps and seeing that I had a seven-hour drive in front of me, I quickly rented a car and hightailed it to Milwaukee. I was sweating bullets through stop and go traffic in Chicago, but I made it to the research facility just in time to moderate those focus groups. If I hadn't gained an hour because of crossing time zones I would not have made it in time. Just in case I didn't make it, the facility had my discussion guide and was getting one of their moderators familiar with it as a Plan B, but for me it would have been unthinkable to have someone else moderate the groups I had prepared. Now I come in the night before.

For the client observers, I provide a schedule for each day of research and the address of the facility for them to load into GPS. I am typically in touch with my clients a lot in the days leading up to the research, but if it's been a little while I'll send out a day-before-the-research email. My phone number and email are on my research

STAGE 4: Conduct The Research

briefs as well, so clients can reach out if they are having any problems getting there the day of the research.

If a client misses a few minutes of the research, oh well, no big deal—unless the client is bringing the stimuli for the research. I plan it on a case-by-case basis as to who is bringing the stimuli. As the moderator, I need to be familiar with the stimuli ahead of time so I can plan the likely follow-up questions for the respondents after their initial reactions. Sometimes sharing the stimuli ahead of time is handled electronically, and in the case of packaging mock-ups or advertising boards, the client may be finalizing the stimuli and producing it right up to the day before the research.

For the participants, the recruiters ask respondents to arrive at the facility at least fifteen minutes ahead of the scheduled session for check-in, plus they send them a reminder email the day before the groups. If a scheduled respondent isn't present ten minutes or so before the research, the facilities will call their cell phone to check their status.

<u>Setting up materials for the focus room and backroom</u>—Setting up for focus groups has some standard components but can also vary widely depending on the study.

The traditional focus group setting will include a conference table with chairs, with the moderator's chair at the head of the table. The moderator's back should face the one-way mirror the clients are sitting behind. This configuration allows for the clients to be able to see the facial expressions of the consumers as they talk. There is typically an easel, easel pad and markers for capturing highlights of the consumer conversation.

In the backroom, I like to give each client a stack of sticky notes and a permanent marker to jot down interesting consumer feedback as they hear it. I have an easel pad in the backroom for the clients to post their sticky notes. Each focus group should get one easel page for sticky notes. This way, at the end of the study, you will have a nice summary of the most interesting points heard.

Some of the more interesting room set-ups I've had include:

- Setting up workstations in the parking lot accessible via the focus room to have plumbers test blowtorches. From that project I learned that a facility has to have certain liability insurance in place to accommodate some activities.

- Decorating the focus room, foyer, hallway and waiting area of a facility in young-girl-birthday-party style décor in order to help elementary school age girls feel comfortable and happy to be there to talk about clothing.

- A replication of an entire Wal*Mart shelf set of dog beds. The facility handled the shelving, while I received all the boxes of dog beds at my home office. I remember this one with humor because my office was filled wall-to-wall with stacked with boxes of dog beds up to my shoulders for several days before the research, leaving only a narrow path open for me to get to my desk.

- Finding a facility in Atlanta with a focus room large enough, including a large access door, for me to have three riding lawn mowers in the room with six participants, a conference table and me.

- Having minivan owners park adjacent to the focus room so we could spend half the discussion in the focus room and half of it inside the van talking about the van's entertainment system features.

The Client Observers' Role

The main job of the client observers is to **watch, listen and keep an open mind**. Consumers will give you their honest opinions, including the good and the bad. Work with a moderator that you trust to ask the right follow up questions to understand the reasons

STAGE 4: Conduct The Research

behind the consumers' opinions.

As an observer, if you hear something you don't like or have questions about, note it. Moderators are trained to check in with the backroom from time to time throughout the sessions. If you have a question or concern when the moderator checks in, let her know at that time and she will follow up with the respondents in the focus room. My personal preference is to address multiple questions that the backroom has gathered when I check in with them two to three times during a focus group.

Some moderators use instant messaging or even an earpiece to get questions and comments immediately, but I find it useful to give clients a little time to gather and prioritize their questions in the backroom. Often questions are answered naturally in the discussion flow in the focus room. If there are several observers in the backroom, it makes it quicker if one person is the point person to communicate all the questions from the observers to the moderator.

Clients also need to **be present**. Make the most of your exposure to the consumers during the groups. You made the time to observe the research and your organization invested the funds to bring these specific people together to focus on your issues. Empathize with them and try to see from their point of view. You may not even realize it at the time how much you are learning about your consumer, but you will find yourself back in the office, quoting what you heard John Doe saying in this focus group. It can be very influential in your organization, when you can say that you heard it straight from John Doe himself.

The next thing a client should keep in mind is: **the overall trends of the feedback are where the power lies**. Hopefully you are talking with enough people over the course of your study that you can identify trends in what people are saying and notice when certain respondents are outliers.

This does not mean the outlier is wrong. Any one person in a focus group represents many people in the population at large. That outlier opinion may signal a niche market opportunity that you can capitalize on at some point. Or it may indicate a vocal minority you should be aware of.

When you quote what you heard from John Doe, it's important to the business that you are clear on what segment of the broader population he represents. It's easy to hear the respondents who agree with your point of view. **You have to work just a little harder to honestly consider what opposing opinions mean to your business.**

Finally, try not to laugh or talk too boisterously behind the one-way mirror. Murmuring is fine, but respondents will hear loud noises and will be more self-conscious about their answers if they are reminded that other people are watching.

<u>What to listen for</u>—Listen not only to what the respondents say, but also to what they don't say and **watch how they act**. Are there issues you thought they would bring up but didn't? Notice how strongly they react or provide feedback. If it's passionate, notice that. If the moderator has to ask question after question to draw out a particular answer, notice that too. Maybe that issue isn't as important as you thought it was to consumers.

Also, as an observer, you'll have a profile of the respondents for reference. The profile will show the participants' answers to the screener survey, including their demographic information and other qualifications for the study. Matching what you hear from the respondents to what you know about their background can help identify additional insights.

<u>Notes on the dress code for observers</u>—don't wear or carry anything in the research facilities that identifies your organization. In most research the moderator is independent and identifies herself that way to the respondents so participants don't feel self-conscious and don't self-edit for the benefit of the company whose product or service is being discussed.

Prepare for sitting in a dark and often cool-temperature room for many hours. Business casual is usually appropriate attire, but can

STAGE 4: Conduct The Research

differ depending on the client's organizational culture.

Sitting for hours cools your body temperature so you may want to bring a sweater or jacket. In most facilities the temperature for the focus room and the observation room are controlled by the same thermostat, which doesn't make any sense. People talking and moving around the focus room are naturally going to feel a lot warmer than observers in a dark room with a few people sitting still.

I hope that you will find a day of focus groups to be as fun and interesting as I do! It's not often that you get to watch your consumers talk in-depth about your product or service. If you're observant, you can usually pick up many insights *far beyond* just the ones you need to meet your research objectives.

STAGE 5:
Analyze and Share The Research Results

Take advantage of the energy created in the fielding of the research to analyze and share the research results quickly and in a way that will have the most impact on decision makers.

The Brand Marketer's Guide to the 5 Stages of Focus Group Research –
STAGE 1: Write the Research Brief
STAGE 2: Recruit the Participants
STAGE 3: Develop the Discussion Guide and Stimuli
STAGE 4: Conduct the Research
STAGE 5: Analyze and Share the Research Results

The main benefit of analyzing and sharing the results of the research is to get everyone on the same page about trends that were discovered while conducting the research. This chapter will provide tips and tricks on report writing. Often the moderator will write the report, but it is likely the market research, brand, or marketing manager who has the ultimate responsibility for sharing the information within their organization.

Capturing the insights in a report will help the audience see the bigger picture in context of all the feedback received during the study. It's easy for team members to observe one or two outspoken research respondents and take their word as the "truth." Summarizing the results will help draw the focus of the management team to the overall feedback relating to the research objectives.

STAGE 5: *Analyze and Share The Research Results*

Know your audience when sharing the research results

Since the whole point of consumer research is to increase an organization's knowledge of its consumers, the consumer insights have to be **shared in a way that is relevant to the particular organization**. In a sense, the research might as well not have happened until the insights are summarized and shared.

It's critical to know your audience. Determine whether this is a team that will respond better to a Word summary, a PowerPoint report, or a video of the highlights from the research. Debrief with the clients who attend the research and, once the report is finished, if possible, present the findings to the broader team of interested parties back in the client's office.

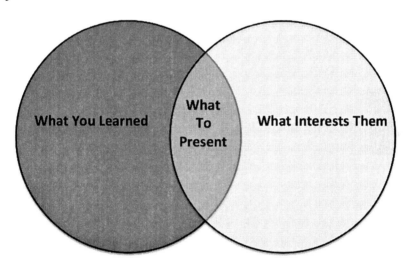

Benefits of sharing the research results quickly

Just picture what could happen if you didn't analyze and share the research results quickly… The VP, who attended one of the six focus groups you did, could choose one thing that one consumer said, then repeat that phrase all over the office. Now your research would be reduced to one factoid, and there's no guarantee it would represent the majority opinion of what you learned. To avoid this, **get out in front of it and lead the management conversation**.

How to analyze and share the research results

1. **Immediately following the last focus group in the study, the moderator should debrief with the client team involved in fielding or observing the research**. Make sure you discuss overall feedback to each research objective.

   Many times you'll start to hear a lot of the same things across multiple groups—that's good! Consistency will give you confidence that you have truly uncovered a trend. The hardest debriefs are ones where the consumer feedback was not consistent across groups. If possible, identify the consistent trends and note the interesting outliers.

   It will make the final debrief go more smoothly and quickly if you've been doing **speedy debriefs after each research session throughout the study**. The big debrief doesn't usually hold many surprises. Instead it reinforces for the whole team what has been heard across the groups.

   Someone should be designated to summarize the final client debrief **by the next day**. Whoever it is, and it's often the moderator, should forgo perfection for the speed of getting the key learnings to the client as soon as possible. If you were there for all of the research, the majority of what is top of mind for you as the research closes will likely be very close to the key learnings you decide to use in the final report.

2. **Write a summary document of the feedback you heard**. Again, this piece is often done by the moderator, but could also be done by a designated observer. There are even people who can be hired

STAGE 5: Analyze and Share The Research Results

just to write the report. They watch the videos and then summarize the information in a written report.

For this, I like to refer back to the objectives of the research and make sure each objective is addressed. Also be sure the summary speaks to the sentence "The results of this research will be used to…" from the original objectives.

Even when I know I'm going to do a final report in presentation format, I find it helpful to write out the details in regular document format and then summarize them into bullet points for slides as a summary step.

I like to address several key points:

- What was surprising about what the consumers said?

- Did the feedback confirm the ingoing hypotheses? If not, how should the business team think differently about the topic?

- Did one segment of consumers give different feedback from the others? Does something specific to this segment of consumers need to be done with the product, packaging or messaging?

3. **Create a presentation highlighting the overall trends** and fleshing out the details of the research. The presentation will formalize the insights learned in the research, as well as illustrate the thoughts and feelings of the research participants with quotes, graphs, and photos.

    My reports tend to run 25-30 slides long, plus any relevant appendix items. Be sure to show in the report any stimuli used in the groups. Since business is constantly evolving, it's very helpful to be able to see the context for the point in time of the research.

Don't forget to **include an executive summary up front** that touches on the learnings that will affect imminent business decisions. Even with the best intentions, many senior leaders may only be able to get to the first few pages.

The final report will also serve as the archive of the whole project. It should include the background, objectives, methodology, summary of important consumer feedback, and implications or recommendations based on those insights.

Also consider including a statement of methodology, reiterating for the audience of the report that focus groups are *qualitative* research. Focus groups can help understand consumers' perceptions, opinions, beliefs and attitudes. *Quantitative* research is needed to gain statistically significant data that can project across a large population what consumers will do in reaction to a particular stimulus, such as a new product, advertisement, package design, etc.

Think of the final report as the final product you are delivering to your client, whether you are the moderator delivering a report to a contracting client or you are a client who will be sharing this report with others in your organization. Taking the time to develop a top-notch final report you can be proud of will always be worth the effort.

And There You Have It

I hope this book has given you the information you need to approach focus group research with an understanding of how to conduct successful focus groups. The five stages presented here are the ones I consistently use with my clients.

As a consumer brand marketer I managed and watched focus groups for ten years, and learned what I liked and didn't like in a moderator. For the past ten years, I have been honing the craft of qualitative research consultant myself. I've filled these pages with all the best how-to tips I've garnered over the years and I hope they serve you well.

Understanding consumers' perspectives through focus groups or other market research will help business leaders excel in their own careers by allowing them to create products, services and messages that best meet consumers' needs and desires.

Acknowledgements

Thank you to my friends and colleagues who took the time to read and comment on my manuscript. Your valuable feedback has enhanced the quality of this book immeasurably. I appreciate your time and support!

- **Miriam Bogard**, Designer at Shelf Genie, Organizing Queen
- **Heather Carlisle**, Vice President Client Services, Moasis
- **Michelle Claravall**, Menu Innovation Manager, McDonald's Corporation
- **Dana Conover**, Former Director Marketing, Innovation, Elmer's Products
- **Ruth Connolly**, Clarity Research LLC
- **Cindy Dyer**, Former Director Market Research, Abbott Nutrition
- **Lisa Greene**, Former Vice President Marketing, Scotts Miracle-Gro
- **Megan Hand**, Copy Editor, Piano Teacher, Photographer, Author
- **Jennifer Hanley**, Former Sr. VP Brand Marketing, Nationwide Insurance
- **Marty Johnson**, MJ Dynamics, Retired
- **Donna Kozik**, Book Writing and Marketing Coach
- **Kendall Nash**, VP Qualitative Research Services, Burke, Inc.

- **Lisa Singer**, Brand Manager, Abbott Nutrition

- **Maya Schmid**, Former Marketing Director, The Coca-Cola Company, Mexico

- **Ray Thomson**, Executive Vice President Global Marketing, Huffy Bicycles

- **Ruth Thomson**, Volunteer and Aunt (no relation to Ray)

- **Holly Vessels**, Woman of Many Talents and Sister-in-Law

- **Stephanie Wolfe,** Facility Director, Focus Pointe Global, Columbus location

Thanks to QRCA, the Qualitative Research Consultants Association, and its many members who have contributed to my knowledge of qualitative research and how to run a successful independent consulting practice.

I would like to thank RIVA Training Institute for providing my formal focus group moderator training and further inspiring my enduring curiosity—in everything.

I would also like to thank all the marketers and market researchers I've worked with over the years at DMB&B, Campbell Soup Company and Scotts Miracle-Gro. I enjoyed the camaraderie and appreciated all the learning.

And I'll close with a thank you to my clients. I am grateful for the opportunity to serve you as a marketing and market research consultant. I love the variety of topics and people you have introduced me to and the experiences we've shared.

Resource List

Qualitative Research Consultants Association (QRCA) is a wealth of information on all facets of qualitative research. You can find them online at www.qrca.org.

For a more complete **guide to focus group activities**, read *Moderating to the Max: A Full-tilt Guide to Creative, Insightful Focus Groups and Depth Interviews* by Jean Bystedt, Siri Lynn and Deborah Potts, Ph.D.

For more **insights on conducting focus groups** from one of the qualitative research industry greats, read *Secrets of a Master Moderator* by Naomi Henderson, CEO of RIVA Market Research and Training Institute.

For a great **guide to writing the participant screener questionnaire**, refer to *The Complete Guide to Writing Questionnaires: How to Get Better Information for Better Decisions* written by David F. Harris.

For **qualitative research consultant or focus group moderator training**, contact RIVA at www.rivainc.com or Burke Institute at www.burkeinstitute.com.

For **step-by-step instructions on marketing concept writing**, read *Marketing Concepts That Win! Save Time, Money and Work Crafting Concepts Right the First Time* by Martha Guidry.

Bonus Content

It's Showtime: Preparing For Your First Day of Focus Groups

By: Ruth Connolly, Clarity Research LLC

It's the night before the first leg of your focus groups. You flew in a day early to make sure a flight delay wouldn't prevent you from being at your first group. By the end of the week you will have been to three different markets, taken six flights, and viewed 12 focus groups across the country. But tonight you are anxious and can't sleep. You plan on arriving at the facility by 11:00 am to meet with your moderator and the rest of your team. That gives you a full hour to prepare before the respondents arrive for the first group. You have the concepts, prototypes and stimuli for the groups. You have ten copies of the discussion guide for the backroom. You poured through the respondent profiles, and know the first names of all the recruited respondents, as well as their gender, income and age. You also know which ones you plan to pay and send if they all happen to show up. Yet you are still restless, wondering what else you could have done to make sure your research gets off to a good start...

Whether you are brand manager, a marketing research project director or a moderator, it's likely that you have felt this way the night before conducting your focus groups. After weeks of careful planning, things seem to be falling into place for your focus groups to run smoothly. But you wonder what else could have been done to ensure the success of your research project.

One important aspect of the focus group methodology often overlooked is Backroom (or viewing room) Management. Choosing the right facility and the right moderator is crucial and helps ensure that the groups and respondents will be handled professionally, but managing the viewers behind the mirror is the key to getting the most out of your focus groups.

Point of Contact

Sometimes the focus group viewing room is packed chock full of people interested in hearing from the consumers. Other times there might be just a handful of key stakeholders who are able to be present. Occasionally there are some present in the backroom while others are viewing remotely through a video streaming service like FocusVision. Regardless of how many attend the focus groups, it is important to designate one person to be the point of contact and spokesperson for the backroom. If you are reading this book, it is very likely that the designated person in the viewing room is you! I want to share with you the key responsibilities of the backroom point of contact to help you execute your research project as flawlessly as possible.

The backroom point of contact has several responsibilities:

- Communicate to the facility any Day of Research needs

- Backroom Etiquette: communicate your expectations of all focus group attendees in the viewing room

- Communicate with the moderator before, during, and after the focus group

- Conduct any necessary pre-briefings and debriefings

It's Showtime: Preparing For Your First Day of Focus Groups

The backroom point of contact is typically the person who is most familiar with the project, understands the research objectives, and is comfortable taking leadership of the viewing room, regardless of who might be in attendance. That is, if CEOs and presidents will be in the backroom watching the focus groups, a junior project manager may not feel comfortable leading the briefings and may defer to someone with more experience. Regardless, the designated backroom point of contact should let the moderator and the facility hostess know that any information, questions, requests should come through them.

Day Of Research Needs

Facilities usually make it very easy to communicate what is needed when you arrive at the facility; many have a form titled 'Day of Research Needs' that they email to you the week prior to the first day of groups. Others may call you and make sure they know exactly what you might need when you arrive at their facility. A few things you want to be sure to communicate to the facility:

- Let the facility know how many backroom viewers you expect, and what time you expect them to arrive.

- Make sure that the viewing room is large enough to accommodate all who plan to attend. Some backrooms are small and can only accommodate a limited number of viewers; others have spacious backrooms with plenty of seating for a large crowd.

- If your backroom guests plan to come at different times or to different groups, let the facility know this, so that there is a hostess at the front to greet any of your later arrivals.

- Let the facility know the names of all research attendees, and whether or not they should check IDs. Most facilities will check the IDs unless you instruct them otherwise.

There are a number of other requests that you might consider for the Day of Research:

- Special food requests/any food allergies
- Respondent food/sandwich trays (especially for groups conducted around dinner time)
- Snacks; in the viewing room, and maybe for the focus group room as well
- Supplies for the focus group room (flip charts, markers, Post-Its, glue sticks, etc.)
- Supplies for viewers (flip charts, different colors of Post-Its, Sharpie markers, etc.)
- Any copies to be made
- Any deliveries to the facility for the research (let them know expected delivery date and number of packages; confirm that shipments arrive and check contents to avoid surprises the day of the groups)
- Videographer, if you want video that pans to each respondent, useful when pulling video clips
- Stationary video/standard DVDs; audio files
- How much time is needed after the last group of the day for a debrief. If you plan to stay an hour after the group and debrief, let the facility know so they can staff appropriately.

Backroom Etiquette

Most backroom attendees are wonderful, engaged people who are attentive to the focus group session, take copious notes, and quietly observe the focus group as it unfolds, drawing useful insights

It's Showtime: Preparing For Your First Day of Focus Groups

from the consumers. They record beautiful quotes from the respondents on their Post-It notes, write down follow-up questions for the moderator, and capture key ideas and opportunities. They are quiet as they sit in the dark, respectfully considering the comments from each and every respondent with unconditional positive regard.

But occasionally, there is that guy who shows up in the backroom, hoping for a free meal and an endless supply of M&Ms. He has a crush on one of the design team members, a young lady who is there to observe her first ever focus group. Behind the mirror, he flirts shamelessly, makes fun of the consumers and how they are dressed, makes fun the moderator and how she looks like a bobble-head doll as she acknowledges one respondent after the other. He laughs loudly, wears a bright neon shirt with the company logo, and when he finally sits down, he begins checking e-mails and shopping on Amazon. He writes a ridiculous question to send in to the moderator to probe more on dental hygiene with the respondent who is missing a front tooth. He laughs so loudly at his own jokes that the moderator hears him and turns around to glare at him through the one-way mirror. If only someone had given him a gentle reminder of backroom etiquette, maybe he wouldn't have made such a spectacle of himself!

The moral of the story is, make sure you let your backroom guests know what is expected of them, and give them the following guidelines so they can be productive attendees and you can get the most out of your research dollars:

Backroom Viewer Guidelines:

- Arrive on time, preferably an hour before the first scheduled group so you are not arriving at the same time as the respondents.

- Dress appropriately, in darker clothing so you are less visible behind the mirror

- o Avoid wearing anything with the company logo, keep badge/ID out of sight
- o Be prepared to show ID to enter the backroom
- o Check in at the facility front desk as an observer/backroom guest. Be mindful of any respondents who may be seated in the waiting area

- Be present and engaged

- o Avoid distractions and pay close attention to the focus group.
- o Take notes, and use a listening guide if one is provided; otherwise follow along with a copy of the discussion guide
- o Keep the research objectives in mind as you take notes
- o Record any salient quotes that you would like to see in the report
- o Write down any additional questions for the moderator and give them to your backroom point of contact.

- Speak quietly at all times to avoid being overheard by respondents
- Be prepared to stay for a debrief after the last focus group

Communicating With Your Moderator

You probably have, by this stage in the game, established a good working relationship with your moderator. You have spent the last couple of weeks fine tuning the discussion guide, and maybe you have used this moderator in the past and are comfortable with their style. Even so, it is good to communicate your expectations from the moderator for the day of your research.

It's Showtime: Preparing For Your First Day of Focus Groups

- Meet with the moderator an hour before the first group to make sure your moderator has everything needed for the group and for the exercises that are planned in the discussion guide.

- Introduce your moderator to everyone in the backroom; let the moderator knew who each person is, and what is their contribution (why are they there listening to these focus groups)

- Spend a few minutes with the moderator and your team walking through the discussion guide. Usually there are no changes in the guide at this point, but this final check of the guide will help familiarize everyone with the line of questioning, and is a good way to check that the moderator has all the proper stimuli (and enough copies of each) for the group.

During a typical focus group, toward the end of the session, your moderator will step out of the focus group and come to the backroom for any follow-up questions. Rather than several people in the backroom bombarding the moderator with additional questions, the point of contact (probably you!) should collect the questions ahead of time and confirm that they haven't already been answered during the discussion. Moderators often think of the same question and may have already asked, even if it was not written into the discussion guide. Keep in mind that, depending on when the moderator comes back, there may only be time for a few key follow-up questions. Make sure these questions tie back to the research objectives and are not redundant. Also make sure you are not adding more questions than the remaining time allows. Any additional questions that are not adequately covered in the first group can be included in the next group, if the question still applies.

After the first group concludes, be sure to thank your moderator first, and then address anything you would like to change for the next group. If there are exercises that don't seem to be working, let the moderator know, so the technique can be adjusted, or a different exercise used that might work better.

If there is any time between the first and second group, it may be helpful to have a quick debrief. If not, make sure your moderator is planning to debrief at the end of the day, after the last group. A debrief is very important, and should not be skipped because it is late in the day or because the backroom attendees want to leave. Not everyone hears and retains everything during a lively group, and this includes the moderator. A debrief doesn't have to be lengthy, and it can greatly enhance the learning and insights.

Conducting a Debrief

The debrief is usually lead by the moderator but could also be led by the point of contact in the backroom, or any other key stakeholder who was present for all groups that day. The debrief session should include everyone from the backroom. To give the backroom attendees a change of scenery, you may want to bring them into the focus group room after all the respondents have left. You can also ask the facility hostess to record the debrief session. The following suggestions will help you conduct a productive debrief:

- Bring any notes, quotes, flip charts from the backroom that you might want to reference during the debrief session.

- Write the research objectives on a flip chart or dry erase board.

- Ask what were the big ah-ha's of the day – what did you learn that was new or different? Anything you heard that was surprising or unexpected?

- What, if anything, was confirmed in these groups? Did anything you heard support current hypotheses?

- Were there any prominent themes? That is, anything you heard that was interesting and was consistent from group to group?

It's Showtime: Preparing For Your First Day of Focus Groups

- o   Any ways that the groups differed from each other?

- What were the top five take-aways from these groups?

The beauty of structuring a debrief session this way is that even if the moderator conducted a marathon session of four groups back-to-back, he or she can still muster up the energy and enthusiasm to easily lead a debrief because the backroom participants are the ones primarily responsible for the content. This also helps align everyone on what was heard during the groups, as well as what wasn't heard. A good debrief helps solidify some of the key insights and provide direction to the moderator or report writer.

Managing a qualitative research project from start to finish can be stressful, and jitters the night before are to be expected. But you can rest assured that if you communicate your needs to the facility and to your moderator, set forth your expectations from your backroom attendees, and allowed ample time for briefings, your research will go as planned.

If you are reading this to prepare for your first, or next qualitative project, I hope that you found this useful in planning your big first day of focus groups. Relax and enjoy as your consumers open up and yield incredible insights to you and your team!

Eleven Things a Client Should Watch for from Focus Group Participants – and Seven Things to Avoid

By: Marty Johnson, MJ Dynamics, Retired

These guidelines may be helpful for first-time observers to a focus group and a refresher for veteran listeners. As an observer, your objective is to understand the group's answers to your questions. These suggestions are intended to help you listen for understanding.

Things To Watch For

1. Familiarize yourself with the guide. It provides an overview of the topics and their importance.

2. Take notes arranged by topic or issue. This is an excellent way to absorb the participants' ideas. Make a separate section for "ah-ha's" or surprises. Challenge yourself to listen for new thoughts and ideas in addition to confirming what you may already know or believe. You might even want to use two different pens to take notes: one for verbatim comments, and another for the ideas that they trigger.

Eleven Things a Client Should Watch for

3. Turn off your internal censors: accept criticism from the participants. Practice *Unconditional Positive Regard* while listening to the participants. The concept was introduced by psychotherapist Carl Rogers.

4. Listen to what everyone has to say, especially the quiet ones. It's easy to think that an outspoken, articulate, or loud respondent represents the group's opinion; however, this may not be the case. The moderator will make every effort to draw out the quiet ones, but overdoing that effort can be embarrassing to them. Some individuals are more naturally reticent than others. However, sometimes, still water runs deep.

5. Look for patterns: of acceptance, of rejection, of intensity. Watch body language and facial expressions. Watch how participants react to other participants' comments.

6. Listen to the language that respondents use to express themselves. They usually don't use the same terminology as people in your industry, and it is insightful to understand how they refer to your product/service/issues.

7. Pay attention to the emotional level of the respondents, both in the way they express themselves verbally, and in their facial expressions and body language. This is a major value of focus groups; you can't tap this information in a survey.

8. Silences, gaps, gasps and other vocal utterances, and confusion are all relevant information. If respondents have questions or incorrect information, focus groups are not necessarily the place to educate them. Respondents are educating us; their lack of knowledge or confusion provides useful information.

9. Listen for *unaided* issues, i.e., top-of-mind concerns that the moderator has not yet mentioned. These issues may be particularly important.

10. Keep in mind the Discussion Guide was carefully prepared is just that, a *guide*. Questions may be reworded and tailored to the immediate understanding of respondents. Topics may not be covered in the same order as the guide. Your moderator will monitor the time, but if an issue is particularly "hot" for respondents, she/he must spend enough time on it, so respondents do not feel ignored. Every effort will be made to cover all the issues on the guide.

11. As you watch and listen, you may wish that your moderator would probe or mention some issue that just occurred to you. Write it down, but listen carefully because it may come up later. Near the end of the session, your moderator will come into the back room to check for additional probes. Via the agreed upon point person, explain simply and quickly what you want to ask. It helps to have the question or topic in written form, and if several observers have questions, to have them all written down. If there are a lot of questions, they must be prioritized as there may not enough time to cover all of them.

Things To Avoid

1. Talking: you cannot listen if you talk.

2. Laughing at participants: the first few moments are awkward for both participants and observers... refrain from making derogatory remarks about participants as it may well color your subsequent perceptions of their behavior. Challenge yourself to find ways in which you are similar to the participants, not different from them – you may be surprised.

Eleven Things a Client Should Watch for

3. Disruptive behavior: loud laughter, thumping tables or the glass, even sending in notes disrupts the flow of the session.

4. Premature conclusions: one comment, in one group discussion, does not necessarily make a marketing truth. As an observer, you are looking for patterns across participants and across groups.

5. Be careful not to dismiss the opinions of the inarticulate, misinformed, or seemingly non-insightful respondents. These people are part of your constituency.

6. Notes to the moderator during the session are distracting, often cause respondents to think they've said something wrong, and can impede the momentum and spontaneity of the group. Please avoid them. Agree ahead of time on "back room checks" at appropriate times throughout the discussion.

7. Under no circumstances should a respondent be pulled from the group by anyone other than the moderator. If there are concerns about a respondent's qualifications, please send a note to your moderator to come to the back room to discuss it.

Enjoy the Research, And Good Listening!

Partnering with your Moderator for Maximum Success

By: Kendall Nash, VP Qualitative Research Services, Burke, Inc.

Any good recipe allows for some degree of flexibility. You can put in a bit more of this or a little less of that to your taste, and the outcome is generally still good. However, there are those few key ingredients that you have to get just right or else the dish is off. When I get it wrong, my family is coincidentally "not that hungry tonight" and leave their plates mostly full.

When it comes to Qualitative Research, there are a few key ingredients that make or break the success of the project: 1) getting the right research participants in the room, 2) involving a moderator who is capable of eliciting the truth from participants, and 3) the moderator and research team working in concert to unveil the richest possible insights. Many teams focus on nailing the first two and neglect to invest in the relationship with the moderator. This dynamic, in particular, is the special sauce that can make good research great.

Strong moderators have an ability to build rapport with participants and connect with them as human beings, have a broad toolkit of techniques to draw from (and an ability to identify the occasions to reach in the bag and pull out the right technique), know the brand's business or do their homework to be versed*, and are able to connect with the brand team in order to know when and where to dig in during conversation with research participants. *(*Note: Moderators* *need not be fully immersed in your category or a specific focus in order to do an effective job digging in for insights. However, they will need to review materials and do their homework in order to effectively communicate with participants and your team.)* Finding the moderator who can deliver on these items still only gets you so far. I've seen strong moderators and seemingly great research that still left the client disappointed.

Moderators who have done this gig for a while can easily point to their most painful or shortchanged projects throughout their career. The common thread? Lackluster dynamics between them and the client team – further magnified when unclear objectives or expectations are sprinkled on top. While there will always be other circumstances influencing the success of a project, working alongside your moderator in the following ways paves a way for smoother projects and richer insights:

Take the time to build chemistry as a team before the research.

Recently I was pulled in on a quick-turn project with a new team I had no history with whatsoever. The clients were racing around on a multitude of projects (a common reality, I totally get it), and had very limited time to meet with our research team prior to launching in the field. While we all hit it off and got along well, we realized there were things we had left on the table during early interviews because we hadn't taken time to build an effective relationship early enough in the process. Learning about each other's work styles and building a productive dynamic are invaluable assets prior to heading into the field. The earlier you can begin developing a relationship (versus being two passing ships "making a project happen"), the richer the project will inevitably be. Once research begins, time during and between groups/interviews is limited. When the moderator and stakeholders are speaking the same language, the moderator is better able to anticipate the needs of the team in order to make discussion with the research participants as fruitful as possible. This solid relationship also makes for swifter and more effective dialogue when the moderator steps out to the backroom for follow-up questions at various points during the research. Every aspect—from consulting on the design, determining who really qualifies to be researched, crafting the discussion guide, conducting the research, all the way through analysis and reporting – the return on investment in building a connection will reap powerful benefits throughout the entire project.

Identify what drives and inspires you, and what keeps you up at night. Make it known.

Recently, while traveling together, a brand manager was discussing some of the realities in his organization that impact how insights are leveraged. As we continued in conversation, he also began mentioning some of his own vision for the brand and organization as a whole. As we headed into interviews the next day, I was able to suggest a couple of additional questions that wouldn't take much real estate in the interview, but could potentially begin paving the way for a future initiative. While we answered the key objectives at hand, the most powerful insights ended up coming from those extra questions, prompted by the context he shared. His willingness and interest in offering me the bigger picture in his mind ultimately changed the trajectory of the brand.

The moderator quickly becomes the primary conduit for a brand's ability to uncover insights that fuel their true business needs. Even the best-intentioned teams often miss sharing background details beyond the primary objectives of the project at hand. Moderators should leverage their skills in uncovering below the surface to more fully understand the context of the decisions their clients are making based on the research. But we can't leave it all to them. Take time before a project launches to reflect on what your personal and organizational motivations are, what keeps nagging at you, and how you could see this research taking your business forward in a meaningful way. Taking the time to share a broader perspective of the business context with your moderator strengthens the level of partnership a moderator is able to provide and offers useful insight from which the moderator can draw from when developing a fine-tuned discussion guide, probing in meaningful ways during an interview, and delivering impactful results that can really penetrate the organization and propel a brand forward.

Build a joint appreciation for the consumer.

"These are the people we serve. It is because of them we get to do what we do every day." One of my favorite clients begins every piece of research we do with a team briefing, in which she not only talks about the research objectives and how to best listen for productive insight gathering, but also as a baseline reminder about the importance and value of the research participants they are about to learn from in the interviews. Most moderators are trained to have unconditional positive regard for everyone interviewed, but building that same level of appreciation together as a team puts everyone in a different mindset for learning. When those in the backroom see their consumers as experts and that it is them they are there to serve, they will hear and observe things in a different and incredibly productive light. This also positively impacts the relationship between the brand team and the moderator. The moderator has just invested themselves in connecting with a participant. When the backroom team not only respects the participants, but also views them as experts central to the success of their business, the discussions between the full research team move into more strategic territory. (Not to say you can't share a smile or two over the unbelievable thing a participant told you about their weekend!)

Build a plan, with flexibility.

Invest in a moderator you trust, and then do just that… trust them. When a client is confident that I really "get" what they want to accomplish and offers me latitude in getting there, I'm much better positioned to get to the level we're trying to go with consumers. Planning ahead and talking through possible scenarios of outcomes is useful. Writing a guide that hits on the topics of interest is good. But always build in flexibility to let the moderator do what they are trained and tuned to do: to flow with the discussion and turn over stones that just may be hiding gold.

Be present.

Recently I experienced an incredibly energizing backroom. Everyone who attended the research came to learn, contribute, and help shape the future of the brand. Conversations were meaningful and when someone shared an idea, everyone in the room was tuned in. We're all moving at a quick pace. Moderators who are agile and able to make needed adjustments on the fly are skilled multi-taskers. They are balancing listening to participants, navigating the conversation to make sure it is productive, anticipating what the brand team may be curious about to probe on, managing time, juggling stimuli and worksheets, and more. Shew! It's no wonder they are buzzing around on research day. And everyone in the backroom has a whole list of to-dos they've carried along on their time away from the office. But it is important everyone on the research team is *present*. This is important every day, but requires intentionality on research day. Moderators and brand teams who are all in – present and fully engaged in the research – are more inclined to land in strategic conversations. Being present improves the ROI on the research tenfold.

Be the champion.

Early in my career I found myself standing in a backroom, uncertain of the next move. I was following a fast-flying conversation and trying to make sense of three different directions that three different people wanted me to take. The group was debating the pros and cons of the approaches but coming up short on consensus given their different vantage points and unique motivations. The tension started growing and I felt myself getting a little clammy. I really needed to get back into the interview. I looked to the person who had been serving as my primary point and he looked as uncertain as I was, and wasn't saying much. Healthy debate in the backroom is a good thing; divergent thinking often results in insightful discussion. But there is a point when the research team leader needs to be the champion for the research, putting politics aside to the extent possible, and guide the moderator in a specific direction.

Listen with your ears and eyes.

Moderators are trained to listen not only to what research participants are saying, but also all the things they are "saying" beyond their words – their tone, demeanor, physical cues, and level of engagement in any given topic. These elements in tandem give us a much more accurate picture of what someone is communicating. Brand teams can contribute in big ways to the research by exercising this same muscle as they observe the research. Being an extra set of eyes and ears to all that is happening during the research can yield to more actionable insights (because lots of heads are better than one!) and builds into the relationship with the moderator as it communicates a sense of *team*.

Building a relationship with your moderator is time and energy well spent. Invest as much in building this connection as you do every other element of the project to optimize your research results. Make your good research great.

Sample Research Brief

BACKGROUND

The Client is developing a clear product as a line extension to its current product. This project includes planning, conducting and reporting on consumer focus groups to guide the continued new product development process.

OBJECTIVES

Consumer Focus Groups:

1. To gauge consumer need and purchase intent (with and without pricing)

2. Learn consumer perceived benefits of the features in order to help create a selling story

3. To gain consumer feedback to the product name

4. To understand consumer reaction to packaging graphics

The results of this research will be used to optimize the Client's clear product innovation and marketing communications.

Sample Research Brief

FOCUS GROUP SPECIFICATIONS

- Date: February 26
- Location: Columbus, OH
- Moderator: Michele Brenner
- Group schedule:

Group	Day / Date	Date / Time	Respondent Description
1	Thursday, 2/26/15	1:00 p.m. to 3:00 p.m.	Moms
2		4:00 p.m. to 6:00 p.m.	Moms
3		7:00 p.m. to 9:00 p.m.	TBD (teachers, office workers or moms group)

  o Recruit 8 per group to seat 6 (participants must have no prior focus group experience with this Client company)

  o In-home use test to be completed after the groups

TIMELINE AND DELIVERABLES

Dates	Tasks	Responsibility
Week 1	Final, approved proposal	Consultant / Client
	Final, approved respondent screener	Consultant / Client
	Begin recruiting	Recruiter
Week 2	Client / Consultant kick-off meeting	Consultant / Client
	Discussion guide outline	Consultant
	Facility logistics (# of observers, directions, food plans)	Consultant / Client

Dates	Tasks	Responsibility
Week 3	Discussion guide feedback	Client
	Final discussion guide	Consultant
	Final stimuli for research	Client
Week 4	Conduct research	Consultant / Client / Recruiter
Week 5	Research summary (Word)	Consultant
Week 6	Final research summary (PowerPoint)	Consultant

FEES AND INVOICING

This project is quoted at $24,000 based upon the above specifications. This includes stationary DVD recordings of the groups. Direct project support charges, including client meals at the research facility, will be billed additionally at cost.

This quote is based on initial communications with the Client. Any significant project specification changes may result in a revised quote. Brenner Brand Marketing will not invoice any changes not communicated in writing and approved by Client Products Inc. until such changes are negotiated.

Brenner Brand Marketing LLC will invoice Client Products Inc. for 50% of the quoted cost upon Client signing this proposal. The final 50% of the total project cost will be invoiced upon completion of the final report. All invoices are payable 30 days from receipt of invoice.

Visit www.focusgroups101.com for FREE example focus group documents to help you take action on the information from this book. You'll find documents such as:
Focus Group Research Cost Breakdown
Participant Screener Specifications
Participant Screener Survey
Discussion Guide Outline
Full Discussion Guide

About The Author

Michele Brenner is the Principal/Moderator for Brenner Brand Marketing LLC, which has been providing marketing consulting and qualitative research to consumer brand marketers since 2005.

Michele's natural curiosity about people, classical consumer packaged goods marketing training, and business management background, combine to make her brand of qualitative research insightful and actionable for the end user. Michele completed the Advanced Moderating course at the RIVA training institute in 2009 and she stays on the cutting edge of research with Qualitative Research Consultants Association training sessions.

Previously a Director of Marketing at Scotts Miracle-Gro, Michele has over a decade of corporate experience growing branded businesses with Scotts Miracle-Gro, Campbell Soup Company and DMB&B (advertising account management on the Clearasil brand for Procter & Gamble). She is known for being results-oriented and effective, having posted double-digit sales and profitability gains for several businesses including V8 Splash and a number of Scotts Turf-Builder lawn care products.

Her career in brand management has given her extensive experience across a broad range of areas, including market research, new product development, project management, team leadership, marketing plan development, brand positioning, advertising development, media planning, package design, customer presentations, pricing, public relations, consumer and trade promotion, P&L management, budgeting, manufacturing, and logistics.

About The Author

Michele earned a Master's Degree in International Management from the Thunderbird School of Global Management in Glendale, Arizona and a Bachelor of Arts in German Area Studies from the University of Oregon in Eugene, Oregon. She lives in Dublin, Ohio with her three children and a menagerie of pets.

Michele's beloved husband of sixteen years, Steve Brenner, passed away unexpectedly in August 2016. She and their children are continuing to live the vibrant lives he would have wanted them to live, while cherishing daily the memory of the great times they had together with him.